Reading First

Eight more practice tests for
the Cambridge B2 First

PROSPERITY EDUCATION
www.prosperityeducation.net

Registered offices: Sherlock Close, Cambridge
CB3 0HP, United Kingdom

© Prosperity Education Ltd. 2023

First published 2023

ISBN: 978-1-915654-06-9

This publication is in copyright. Subject to statutory exception and to the provisions of relevant collective licensing agreements, no reproduction of any part may take place without the written permission of Prosperity Education.

'Cambridge B2 First' and 'FCE' are brands belonging to The Chancellor, Masters and Scholars of the University of Cambridge and are not associated with Prosperity Education or its products.

Cover design and typesetting by ORP Cambridge

For further information and resources, visit:
www.prosperityeducation.net

To infinity and beyond.

Contents

Introduction   5

Test 1   7
Test 2   15
Test 3   23
Test 4   31
Test 5   39
Test 6   47
Test 7   55
Test 8   63
Answer key – Test 1   72
Answer key – Test 2   73
Answer key – Test 3   74
Answer key – Test 4   75
Answer key – Test 5   76
Answer key – Test 6   77
Answer key – Test 7   78
Answer key – Test 8   80

Bonus content

Use of English – Test 1   85
Use of English – Test 2   93

Introduction

Welcome to this second edition of sample tests for the Cambridge B2 First (FCE) Reading examination (Parts 5–7).

Parts 5–7 of the Reading and Use of English section test candidates' ability in reading different types of text for detail, purpose, opinion, tone and attitude, and repeated practice of the assessment format is key to achieving a passing grade.

This resource comprises eight whole Reading tests, answer keys, write-in answer sheets and a marking scheme allowing you to score each test out of 22 marks.

The content has been written to closely replicate the Cambridge exam experience, and has undergone comprehensive expert and peer review. You or your students, if you are a teacher, will hopefully enjoy the wide range of essay topics and benefit from the repetitive practice, something that is key to preparing for this section of the B2 First (FCE) examination.

We hope that you will find this resource a useful study aid, and we wish you all the best in preparing for the exam.

Prosperity Education
Cambridge, 2023

For more Cambridge exam-preparation materials, including free sample tests and online resources, visit www.prosperityeducation.net

Cambridge B2 First Reading

Test 1

Cambridge B2 First Reading

Part 5

You are going to read an extract from a blog in which a man named Hartmann Gumason talks about the World's Strongest Man competition. For questions 31–36, read the text below and decide which answer fits best according to the text. In the separate answer sheet, mark the appropriate answer (A, B, C or D).

Preparing for the World's Strongest Man competition is a demanding process, but it's also a rewarding one. First of all, I have to consume a lot of calories to fuel my training. I usually eat around 8,000 to 10,000 calories per day, relying on a diet that's high in protein-rich foods like lean meat, fish and eggs, carbohydrates and healthy fats. I also have to eat frequently throughout the day to reach my calorie goal, so I'm constantly snacking on things like nuts and berries in between multiple large meals.

Secondly, building up almost super-human strength requires intense weightlifting and functional fitness exercises. I train for several hours a day, six days a week, and I focus on exercises that will help me perform well in the competition. This includes lifting heavy weights.

It's important to take care of your body while training, and I make sure to warm up properly before each workout, stretch regularly and take it easy on the days when I'm feeling particularly tired or sore. At the same time, it's essential to push yourself to reach your goals.

Preparation for the World's Strongest Man competition requires a great deal of dedication, and I've had to give up some of my social life and devote all of my time and energy to training. It can also be difficult to maintain relationships with friends who don't understand the time and dedication required to compete at this level. But I'm lucky, I have a network of people who understand and support my goals.

Training also costs a fortune. There are gym memberships, supplements, and equipment, as well as the high cost of travel from Iceland to many different competition venues and expensive lodging for the competition. I mean, it's great to see the world while I'm competing, but it does come at a price early on, I cut down a lot so I wouldn't miss out. But I have made up my mind to give 100 percent to make it to the competition, and I believe it will be worth it.

Of course, I couldn't do any of this without the support of my sponsors. It's vital to have a solid brand and a strong and constant social media presence. This allows you to showcase your achievements, training and personality to a wider audience, and, for some competitors, attract potential sponsors. I make sure to consistently perform at my best and maintain a positive image, both on and off the competition stage, for the reputation of the sponsors. At the same time, I believe in building and maintaining strong relationships with my sponsors, who I mostly meet at competitions. I keep in touch with them, as, to me, it's crucial to provide regular updates on my training and competition progress, and show my appreciation for their support. By doing this, I am able to keep their interest and ensure that the partnership benefits us both.

If you're curious about being a strongman or preparing for the competition, my advice would be to make up your mind that you're going to commit to the tough training schedule, do your research on the challenges your body will face and consider the costs. You could even start putting some money aside for training or when a competition comes up. Don't forget to share your experiences with your family and friends, and find a supportive community of competitors.

It's not an easy path, but it's incredibly satisfying and the sense of achievement you feel when you step on the competition stage is unmatched. So, go for it, and give it your all!

31 What does Hartmann suggest about his meals?

    A   He tends to stick to strict mealtimes.
    B   He has to regularly calculate his calorie intake.
    C   He has to eat food he doesn't enjoy.
    D   He eats a varied diet to meet his calorie target.

32 What point about his training does he make in paragraph three?

    A   That working hard and resting are equally important.
    B   That training hard can make your body ache.
    C   That warming up and stretching must be done simultaneously.
    D   That resting can only happen when not preparing for a competition.

33 What does Hartmann say about his relationships?

    A   He prefers training to socialising with friends and family.
    B   He can't have friends because of the demands of his training.
    C   He thinks that his family struggles to understand the effort his training requires.
    D   He has a group of people who appreciate his commitment to training.

34 What does Hartmann say about the financial aspects of his lifestyle?

    A   the travel opportunities are what make the costs worth it.
    B   he gave up things in the past to help him in the future.
    C   the accommodation is often the most expensive part.
    D   he nearly gave up because of rising costs.

35 How does Hartmann feel about his sponsors?

    A   His sponsors increases the amount of pressure.
    B   He and his sponsors both see the advantages in their relationship.
    C   His sponsors require him to provide frequent updates on his training.
    D   He can only gain good sponsors and deals through social media.

36 Hartmann's main point in the final paragraph about training and competing is that

    A   it is important to socialise with people with similar interests.
    B   you have to be physically and mentally strong.
    C   it is worth doing despite the sacrifices you have to make.
    D   you need to have enough money before you start competing.

Part 6

You are going to read an extract from an article in which a careers adviser gives advice on choosing a university. Six sentences have been removed. For questions 37–42, read the text below and, in the separate answer sheet, choose from options A–G the sentence that fits each gap. There is one extra sentence that you do not need to use.

Choosing a university

A careers adviser suggests how to choose a university

As a careers adviser, I'm often asked by students about the best way to look for a suitable university course when finishing school. It's a critical decision, and one that can have a significant impact on a person's future, so it's essential to approach the process with careful consideration.

Firstly, I always advise students to look into a variety of courses that interest them but also not to stick to things they know. [37] You might be surprised to find that something that you never thought you'd be interested in could turn out to be a great option for you.

There are subjects available that you might never even have heard of, so it's important to look beyond the school curriculum. [38] You can do anything, and not just the typical subjects you learn at school.

Once you have a list of potential courses, it's time to weigh up the pros and cons of each one. Consider the course content, the reputation of the university, the location and the potential job prospects after graduation. Make a list of these key factors and other things that are most important to you, and use it to evaluate each course on your list.

[39] Unless you have a million pounds in the bank, you'll need to consider the cost of tuition, accommodation and other living expenses. How are you going to get home in the holidays? How much is rent in the student halls or rented houses? Think about how you'll pay for everything and what support might be available to you, such as scholarships or student loans. The university will often have a list of potential sources of funding.

As soon as you've reduced your list to a handful of potential courses, it's time to start doing your research. Attend university open days and information sessions, talk to current students and read up on the course content and requirements. [40] The more you know about each course, the institution and the fees, the easier it will be to make an informed decision.

When it comes to making the final decision, it's essential to trust your instincts. If a course feels like a good choice for you, and you can picture yourself enjoying the subject matter and succeeding in the university environment, it's likely that you've made the right choice. [41] You need to make sure you're making the right decision, because it's a big financial commitment.

Finally, don't be afraid to seek guidance and support from others. Talk to your teachers, parents and careers advisers about your options, and get their advice on how to approach the decision-making process. It can be helpful to get an outside perspective and to discuss ideas with someone who has experience in this area.

Overall, looking for a suitable university course when finishing school is a complex process that requires careful consideration and research. [42] By following these steps, you'll be well on your way to finding the perfect course for you and taking the next step towards a bright and fulfilling future.

Test 1

A It's important to look into a range of courses, think about the positives and negatives of each one, consider the practicalities and do your research.

B On the other hand, you may decide that you want to stick to something you already know, such as history, maths, or a foreign language.

C What about comedy, the science of baking, or oil and gas management, for instance?

D You could also search YouTube, for example, as it's usually possible to find 'day in the life' videos by students at the university you're considering.

E It's also crucial to consider the financial practicalities of each course.

F That way, they can keep an open mind and explore a range of subjects to see what might be a good fit.

G However, if you have any doubts, it's important to listen to those too.

Part 7

You are going to read a newspaper article about a newspaper article about learning a language. Six sentences have been removed. For questions 43–52, read the text below and, in the separate answer sheet, choose the correct paragraph (A–D).

Learning a language

Four people describe how they feel about learning foreign languages

A **Steve:** I've always been fascinated by foreign languages, and I'm finally learning one on my own! It's challenging, but I'm optimistic that I can do it, and I much prefer it to taking lessons. I've found that the best approach is to build up my skills slowly, starting with the basics and gradually adding more complex concepts. To vary things, I like to listen to music and watch movies in the language that I'm learning. This not only helps me practise my listening skills but also exposes me to new vocabulary, and I get to learn about the culture as well. When I find all the learning too much, I take a quick break to recharge, and usually do something different each time. I find walking outside or going to the gym helps me get back my focus and enthusiasm. To me, learning a new language is a great way to expand your horizons and open up new possibilities for work.

B **Borja:** Taking up a foreign language has been a real struggle for me. I find it hard to note down everything the teacher says, and I'm constantly worried about getting things wrong when I hand in my essays and written assignments. It's difficult to make sense of the grammar rules and vocabulary, and I often feel bored to tears during class. Equally, I find it hard to stay motivated when I feel like I'm not making progress. While some people seem to pick up languages easily, I'm finding it very challenging. I don't think it's something that comes naturally to me. I wish I could appreciate the process more, but it feels like hard work. Despite the difficulties, I know that knowing a foreign language can be an incredibly helpful thing for when I go abroad, and I'm determined to push through.

C **Pallavi:** Learning a foreign language has always been a piece of cake for me because I'm great with technology! If you're struggling to pick up a new language, I have some tips that might help from when I was studying and taking lessons. First, look through online resources and apps that can make learning fun and interactive and make notes if you like doing so. Second, set aside specific time each day to practise, and use the same tools and techniques each time to reinforce your learning. Similarly, absorbing yourself in the language by listening to music, watching movies and speaking with native speakers. Finally, don't be afraid to make mistakes! The more you practise, the better you'll get. Practise every day and keep at it, and before you know it you'll be a fluent speaker! It took me a while, but I got there eventually!

D **Adriana:** Learning a new language is something I have always wanted to take up, so I decided to sign up for a course through work. It's been a great way to get into the language and learn more about the culture. To be honest, it's been tricky but also very rewarding. At first, it was challenging to feel confident and keep up with the pace of the group, although I eventually got there. I find that practising regularly and doing activities outside of class helps me to stay on track. So far, I have learned a lot of new vocabulary and grammar, and I am starting to feel more confident when speaking, even though I still make mistakes. Overall, I think that learning a new language is worthwhile, and I am happy that I decided to give it a try. I still have a long way to go before I can consider myself fluent, but I am excited to continue learning.

Which person:

states that learning a foreign language can be a useful skill for travelling?	**43**
finds learning a language to be quite straightforward?	**44**
thinks that learning with others was initially difficult?	**45**
mentions that they do not have a natural ability for languages?	**46**
explains that making errors is part of the learning process?	**47**
thinks that it's essential to develop a routine when learning?	**48**
suggests learning a new language creates employment opportunities?	**49**
believes that they will succeed with their self-study?	**50**
says that extra work in addition to lessons helps them to focus?	**51**
mentions how they feel about written work?	**52**

Answer sheet   Test No. ☐

                                                Mark out of 22 ☐

Name _____   **Date** _____

Part 5   *6 marks*

Mark the appropriate answer (A, B, C or D).

| 0 | A | B | **C** | D |

31	A	B	C	D		34	A	B	C	D
32	A	B	C	D		35	A	B	C	D
33	A	B	C	D		36	A	B	C	D

Part 6   *6 marks*

Add the appropriate answer (A–G).

| 37 | 38 | 39 |
| 40 | 41 | 42 |

Part 7   *10 marks*

Add the appropriate answer (A, B, C or D).

| 43 | 44 | 45 | 46 | 47 |
| 48 | 49 | 50 | 51 | 52 |

Cambridge B2 First Reading

Test 2

Cambridge B2 First Reading

Part 5

You are going to read an extract from an interview in which Sam Godfrey talks about the Young Musician of the Year competition. For questions 31–36, read the text below and decide which answer fits best according to the text. In the separate answer sheet, mark the appropriate answer (A, B, C or D).

My name is Sam Godfrey and I am currently involved in the Young Musician of the Year competition. I first realised that I might have a chance of winning the competition about a year ago when my music teacher and I spoke at a school music festival, and she suggested that I try out for it in front of judges. I was hesitant to apply at first because I knew the competition would be difficult and that the level of talent was going to be extremely high. However, after looking it up online, I decided to try, and I was happy when I found out that I had been selected to compete. It was a great moment when I read the acceptance email; I still can't believe it.

Competing in the Young Musician of the Year competition has been challenging. Honestly, all the other competitors are so good. Every musician here is talented in their own way, and it can be stressful at times to know how to succeed. I have to do everything I can to stand out, and that includes building my brand both online and offline, which I've just begun doing. On the other hand, it's also incredibly inspiring to be surrounded by so much talent and to learn from my peers.

The preparation is hard, but having a routine of sorts definitely helps. It's been a bit of a struggle though, especially since I've been living out of a suitcase for the past few weeks and travelling here, there and everywhere. But I've found ways to stay focused and maintain my routine, even when things get busy. I make time for practice every day, and I always make sure to eat healthily and get enough rest. Additionally, I surround myself with positive people who inspire me.

Winning the competition would be a dream come true. Of course, that is my goal – to take home the grand prize and be crowned the Young Musician of the Year. It would be an incredible achievement and recognition of all the hard work I've put in. But even if that doesn't happen, I want to walk away from this experience having pushed myself to the limits, pleased with myself and the effort I've put in and having grown as a musician. I want to prove to myself and to others that, with hard work and dedication, anything is possible. Whether I win or not, I'll walk away with admiration for every single person that has taken part in this challenging process.

Line 26　It would also be a way for me to share my music with a wider audience and inspire others to go after their passions. Therefore, I hope to use my win as a springboard to help my career progress. I plan to continue writing and performing my original music, and to work with other musicians and artists in the industry. And I want to give back by sharing my experience and offering support to other young musicians.

Ultimately, my objective is to make a meaningful impact on the music world and to be remembered as a talented artist. Winning the Young Musician of the Year competition would be a huge step in the right direction, and I can't wait to see what the future holds.

31 How did the writer become involved with the competition?

- **A** By attending another event.
- **B** By watching something online.
- **C** By asking a friend.
- **D** By asking his teacher to apply for him.

32 In order to be successful in the competition, the writer needs

- **A** to have a strong internet presence.
- **B** to receive an acceptance email.
- **C** to do everything possible to be noticed.
- **D** to read plenty of books.

33 What has made the competition difficult for the writer?

- **A** Not having a schedule.
- **B** Not eating well.
- **C** Not sleeping much.
- **D** Not being based in one place.

34 Winning the competition would make the writer feel

- **A** relieved.
- **B** skilled.
- **C** scared.
- **D** respected.

35 What does 'springboard' mean in line 26?

- **A** A problem to an existing solution.
- **B** Something that requires hope.
- **C** A starting point from which something develops.
- **D** Something that requires a crowd.

36 The writer's main goal is to

- **A** write songs for other musicians and artists.
- **B** influence the music world in a big way.
- **C** create a place to share music.
- **D** become a famous music director.

Part 6

You are going to read a newspaper article in which the success of the Jurassic World movie series is celebrated. Six sentences have been removed. For questions 37–42, read the text below and, in the separate answer sheet, choose from options A–G the sentence that fits each gap. There is one extra sentence that you do not need to use.

A Roaring Success

The Jurassic World movie franchise has been extremely successful since the first film's release in the early 1990s.

The franchise has come up with six movies, each one more thrilling than the last, and has broken free of the traditional monster- movie mould. It owes much of its success to the original book, *Jurassic Park*, written by Michael Crichton in 1990. The novel follows the story of a group of scientists and investors who create a theme park filled with dinosaurs. [37]

The book was a success, but its 1993 cinematic adaptation by Steven Spielberg was iconic.

In the story, the characters try to avoid the dinosaur and escape, but the T-Rex continues to chase them, eventually destroying one of the cars and leaving the characters alone and scared. This scene is famous for the terrifying way in which the T-Rex appears and the impressive special effects that bring the dinosaur to life.

Unsurprisingly, the film was a hit, and it also made a lot of money. [38]

The next films that followed were The Lost World: Jurassic Park (1997) and Jurassic Park III (2001), which similarly feature exciting dinosaur battles and chase scenes that keep viewers on the edge of their seats.

However, the films weren't as successful as the first, so the creators went back to the beginning and early ideas. [39] The film featured larger and more terrifying creatures and was filled with action-packed scenes that left audiences shocked. In one key scene, a storm disables the electric fences and allows the dinosaurs to break free. The T-Rex then attacks the cars carrying the main characters, causing chaos and destruction.

The success of the movie prompted the filmmakers to make a follow-up, and in 2018, Jurassic World: Fallen Kingdom arrived in cinemas. [40]

The movie was a hit with fans, and it made over a billion dollars worldwide. The latest film, Jurassic World: Dominion, ends with dinosaurs living peacefully alongside real-world animals.

What makes the Jurassic World films stand out from other monster movies is its ability to create creatures that feel real, despite their prehistoric origins. [41]

In conclusion, the Jurassic World movie franchise has basically set the standard for modern monster movies. [42] Whether you're a long-term fan of the original Jurassic Park or a newcomer to the franchise, there's something for everyone in the Jurassic World.

Test 2

A Its impact on pop culture will undoubtedly continue to entertain readers and movie lovers for generations to come.

B The filmmakers have used new technology to create creatures that look and move like real dinosaurs, making the movies feel even more fascinating.

C However, this time, the risks were higher – audiences were used to the latest technology so the special effects had to be better than ever before

D The scientific accuracy and attention to detail made it fascinating for both dinosaur enthusiasts and sci-fi fans, making it an instant hit.

E Therefore, it's no surprise that the franchise is so popular.

F Then there were the books, board games, toys and video games, all of which made even more money.

G After a break, the franchise returned with the movie Jurassic World, which ended up being an even bigger hit than the ones before.

Part 7

You are going to read an article in which four people talk about living on an island. Six sentences have been removed. For questions 43–52, read the text below and, in the separate answer sheet, choose the correct paragraph (A–D).

Island life in Scotland

A **Marta:** As a young au pair living on the Isle of Island, this small island in Scotland is simply breath-taking. Compared to my hometown, Islay is a relaxing place, surrounded by stunning natural landscapes. I am constantly amazed by the beauty of this island (when it's not pouring down, of course!) and I feel incredibly grateful to have had the opportunity to live here. Living in a foreign country has definitely been a challenge, but I am so glad that I decided to come here and make this huge change in my life. I signed up for the au pair program as a way to experience a different culture and way of life, and I have not been disappointed. I know that I need to leave soon and return to the real world, but this experience has taught me so much about myself. I will always look back on my time on Islay with fondness and appreciation.

B **Brian:** My wife and I decided to move from the hustle and bustle of life in Glasgow in Scotland to the quiet island of Mull, in the north of the country. We were both feeling stressed, and we knew we needed a change. The demands of the 9–5 were tough, and we needed to find a way to calm down and enjoy life again. However, the move wasn't straightforward. However, the move wasn't straightforward. First of all, we had to cut down on our expenses in order to make this move happen. We knew that we would be paid little compared to our previous salaries, but we were willing to take that chance in order to have a better quality of life. But it was worth it! Life on Mull is much more relaxed, and we have time to appreciate the small things in life and to enjoy the beauty of nature. We have also made some amazing new friends of different ages in the local community.

C **Cameron:** I have always lived on the Isle of Skye, and could never imagine living anywhere else. Sometimes, people suggest that I should consider moving to a bigger city for more job opportunities and a high salary. But the truth is that I couldn't turn down the natural beauty and calmness that Skye provides. Besides, I have been fortunate enough to have found a job that I enjoy and which I can do from home. Obviously, if circumstances change and my job suddenly requires me to travel then I might have to consider leaving, but Skye will always hold a special place in my heart and I know I would be a regular visitor if I did leave. I love hiking and taking long walks, and the island offers stunning views that I know it would take me far longer to find on the mainland. In addition, the sense of 'family' here is incredibly special. Everyone knows each other, and there is a strong support system that is very rare elsewhere. I am grateful to have grown up on this island.

D **Colin:** I live on the small island of Iona, but, to be honest, I can't wait to move away. Don't get me wrong, Iona is beautiful place. But there is not a lot to do for youngsters. Believe me: if you've seen one visitor centre, you've seen them all! I'm still young, so I have to wait a few more years yet, but as soon as I'm old enough I'm moving, maybe to a different country! Some people advise against leaving the island, saying that I'll miss the small community and how quiet life is (I definitely won't!). I feel ready for something new. I've been looking for jobs where I can be a small fish in a big pond for a change. I want to experience new things, meet new people and feel as free as a bird.

Which person:

says that they are tired of seeing the same thing more than once? | 43

compares where they live to another country? | 44

refers to the wet weather? | 45

believes that they would return to visit if they moved away? | 46

mentions earning less money than before? | 47

suggests that they want something more exciting to happen to them? | 48

says that they used to be worried and anxious? | 49

suggests that they don't have much time left on their island? | 50

states that they want to see the rest of the world? | 51

explains how the community is refreshingly different from most places? | 52

Answer sheet　　　　　　　　　　　　　　　　　　　　　　　Test No. ☐

　　　　　　　　　　　　　　　　　　　　　　　　　　　　Mark out of 22 ☐

Name _____　　　　　　　Date _____

Part 5　　　　　　　　　　　　　　　　　　　　　　　　　　　*6 marks*

Mark the appropriate answer (A, B, C or D).

31	A B C D		34	A B C D
32	A B C D		35	A B C D
33	A B C D		36	A B C D

Part 6　　　　　　　　　　　　　　　　　　　　　　　　　　　*6 marks*

Add the appropriate answer (A–G).

| 37 | 38 | 39 |
| 40 | 41 | 42 |

Part 7　　　　　　　　　　　　　　　　　　　　　　　　　　*10 marks*

Add the appropriate answer (A, B, C or D).

| 43 | 44 | 45 | 46 | 47 |
| 48 | 49 | 50 | 51 | 52 |

Cambridge B2 First Reading

Test 3

Cambridge B2 First Reading

Part 5

You are going to read an extract from a magazine in which a woman discusses her fear of flying. For questions 31–36, read the text below and decide which answer fits best according to the text. In the separate answer sheet, mark the appropriate answer (A, B, C or D).

I've been afraid of flying for as long as I can remember. It's a fear that comes over me every time I've had to fly, and it took me a long time to try to figure out the reasons why. It's not the fear of the plane falling into the ocean, the plane moving side-to-side in bad weather or even a relatively common fear of heights, although these do scare me. It's the fear of being trapped, the fear of being out of control, the fear of something going wrong and not being able to get out.

Over the years, I've read books on the subject, I've listened to relaxation tapes with supposed calming voices and sounds, and I've even taken a course specifically designed for people with aviophobia, which is the specific term for a fear of flying. While it was initially a good starting point to talk to others who share my same fear, and it helped in many ways, unfortunately, none of these methods fully worked for me. My fear of flying had only grown stronger with each passing year.

I realised that I needed to find a different approach, so I decided to explore therapy. The therapist suggested that we use a method called 'exposure therapy', which involves gradually exposing me to the fear of flying in a controlled environment.

Our first session involved talking generally about my childhood and my fear of flying, before identifying the specific things that caused it. We discussed the physical sensations I experienced when I felt anxious, such as sweating and shaking, as well as the negative thoughts that raced through my mind. My therapist helped me to understand that my fear was unreasonable and that, statistically, the chances of something going wrong on a flight were incredibly low.

Line 19   In the following sessions, we started, in small steps, to face the fear. First, we looked at pictures of planes and airports, then we went on to visit an airport and spoke to a pilot, and, finally, we took a short domestic flight. Each step of the way, my therapist talked me through ways to manage my anxiety and taught me techniques for relaxation and mindfulness that I could do at home.

After months of working together, I felt ready to take a more significant step. I booked a long flight to Europe, something that I never thought I would be able to do. The lead-up to the flight was challenging, and I experienced a lot of anxiety, but I was determined to face my fear.

On the day of the flight, I arrived at the airport early, so I had plenty of time to get through security and settle in before the flight. I used techniques I'd been working on for a while – things my therapist had taught me – to manage my anxiety, including deep-breathing and positive self-talk. I also took medication to help me relax.

The flight was long and challenging, but I made it through. I experienced moments of anxiety, but I was proud of myself for facing my fear and not giving up. When I arrived at my destination, I felt a sense of achievement that I had never experienced before.

Now, a few years later, I still experience some anxiety when I fly, but I manage it much better. I've continued to work with my therapist, and we've even taken another flight together. I've also learned to be more aware and present when I travel, focusing on the sights and experiences around me rather than my fear.

Overcoming my fear of flying and going to therapy have been among the most challenging things I've ever done. However, it's also been one of the most rewarding experiences. I've learned that I'm stronger than my fear. I also feel more confident in myself and my abilities. While I may never love flying, I now know that I can face it and come out the other side.

Test 3

31 What does the writer say she's afraid of when flying?

　　A　being unable to escape if something bad happens

　　B　the plane crashing into the water

　　C　the rough air caused by thunderstorms

　　D　being in a high place

32 In the second paragraph the writer says that

　　A　she hadn't ever tried to deal with her fear of flying.

　　B　sharing her fear of flying with others helped her to some extent.

　　C　her fear of flying got worse when she knew it had an official name.

　　D　listening to tapes helped her calm her mind and rest.

33 What did the writer's therapist help her to realise in her first sessions?

　　A　That the fear had started from a specific moment in her past.

　　B　That her anxiety produced only mental reactions.

　　C　That data suggested her fear was illogical.

　　D　That physical responses were harder to control.

34 What was the main focus of the 'following sessions' in line 19?

　　A　Talking with an airline captain about her fear.

　　B　Studying images related to her fear.

　　C　Being gradually exposed to the fear.

　　D　Learning to be cautious of the fear.

35 What does the writer say about her flight to Europe?

　　A　She had been practising strategies to help her in this moment.

　　B　Her medication was more beneficial than other techniques.

　　C　She experimented with new techniques to help her relax.

　　D　Her therapist suggested that arriving early would help her feel calm.

36 How does the writer feel about trying to overcome her fear of flying?

　　A　She believes that she'll probably enjoy flying more in the future.

　　B　She says that the challenges of therapy almost made her give up.

　　C　She thinks that the benefits outweigh the difficulties she faced.

　　D　She believes that she can overcome the other fears in her life.

Part 6

You are going to read an extract from a newspaper in which a person talks about public transport improvements. Six sentences have been removed. For questions 37–42, read the text below and, in the separate answer sheet, choose from options A–G the sentence that fits each gap. There is one extra sentence that you do not need to use.

Making Public Transport Attractive

How are governments innovating to improve the use of public transport in cities?

Governments around the world are thinking up new ways to encourage their citizens to use public transport as a way to reduce traffic congestion, air pollution and carbon emissions. **37**

In many cities, people still settle for using their cars as their primary mode of transportation, despite the heavy traffic and high costs associated with this. **38** There are many different ways in which they are doing this.

One example of a government actively promoting public transport is the London Congestion Charge, a fee that drivers must pay to enter the city centre during peak hours. It was first introduced in 2003 as a way to reduce traffic congestion and improve air quality in the city. **39** The introduction of the charge was controversial, with many drivers and businesses opposing it. However, it has been successful in reducing traffic congestion and improving air quality, and it has become a model for other cities around the world. The charge has seen several changes over the years, including an increase in the fee and expansion of the charging zone. It remains a key part of London's transportation policy, and its success has helped to form transportation policy in other cities around the world.

Commuters are more likely to switch if they make a trip on public transport and find that it is good value for money, or find out that it operates 24–7, making it easier to get around.

Therefore, many governments are investing heavily in improving their public transport systems. Tokyo has one of the most advanced and efficient public transport systems in the world, and the city continues to build on its success. One of the most significant improvements in recent years was the introduction of the Tokyo Skytree, a new high-speed train that can take commuters from central Tokyo to the Skytree Tower in just a few minutes. The city also introduced a new mobile app called Navitime that provides real-time information on train schedules and delays, making it easier for commuters to plan their journeys. **40** These improvements have made Tokyo's public transport system even more efficient and convenient for commuters and tourists alike.

41 For instance, Paris has one of the most successful bike-sharing schemes in the world. Introduced in 2007, it has since become a model for other cities around the world. The *Vélib'* scheme provides more than 14,000 bicycles at 1,230 stations throughout the city, making it easy for people to rent a bike for short trips. **42**

In conclusion, governments are actively trying to encourage people to use public transport by investing in its systems, discussing the benefits of public transport, and introducing interesting new services and technologies. By making it more convenient and attractive, people will be more likely to choose public transport instead of using their cars. This will result in a cleaner, more efficient and longer-lasting transportation system.

A However, governments are now asking its citizens to avoid using their cars and make a journey on public transport instead.

B In addition, this busy city continued to invest in its subway system, introducing new trains and increasing the frequency of service during peak hours.

C Other governments are also coming up with new ideas and introducing new technologies and services that make public transport more convenient and attractive.

D They are also testing out different strategies to improve public transport, making it more reliable, efficient and convenient for people travelling to and from work.

E Only time will tell if these efforts of governments will change people's minds and encourage them to choose greener, more sustainable public transport options.

F At the time, this famous city was one of the most crowded in Europe, with long traffic delays and high levels of air pollution.

G Overall, this project has been a great success for the city and has helped to promote a culture of cycling.

Cambridge B2 First Reading

Part 7

You are going to read a newspaper article about growing old gracefully. Six sentences have been removed. For questions 43–52, read the text below and, in the separate answer sheet, choose the correct paragraph (A–D).

Growing old: The importance of health and well-being

A   **Ernest:** Keep active! I have always done some form of physical exercise, and I cannot stress enough the importance of keeping active. Even now, as an armchair sportsman, I still try to keep active as much as possible. One of the best ways to keep active is to make the most of the physical activities that you enjoy. If you love to dance, join in with a local dance class or sing along with a choir. If you enjoy playing games, find a game that involves moving your body. As well as being a great form of exercise, being active can also help you to stay socially connected and improve your mental health. For me, I make an effort to swim twice a week. Swimming is easy on the joints, and it gets the blood moving. It is never too late to start a new activity, and finding something that you enjoy can be the key to staying active and healthy in your later years.

B   **Mary:** One of the most important lessons I have learned is that we should focus on the things that make us feel good, both physically and mentally. For me, starting yoga again in my sixties was amazing, and I have found that regular exercise and stretching have helped me to maintain my flexibility and ability to move. I still go to a class every week. However, it's not just physical health that is important as we age. Mental health is just as crucial, and I have found that practising mindfulness is an excellent way to keep my mind sharp and focused. It helps me to reduce stress and anxiety and improve my overall sense of well-being. It has also taught me that if something brings negativity into your life, be it a relationship, a job, or a habit, it's important to cut it out and focus on the things that bring you joy and happiness.

C   **Pepe:** One of my favourite sayings is 'A little of what you want does you good', and I believe that this applies to life as well. We don't have to give up everything that we enjoy as we get older, but we do need to learn to take things at a more relaxed pace. It's all too easy to get caught up in the rush of everyday life, but taking the time to slow down and live through each moment can make a big difference to our overall sense of well-being. I have always been incredibly grateful for the simple pleasures in life, such as spending time with my three young grandchildren, reading a good book or simply enjoying a cup of tea. Although it's true that our bodies and minds may not be as strong as they once were, we can still find joy. For me, one of the best things I did was restarting the piano lessons I had given up when I was 14. It's not been easy, but with the help of the many tutorials on the internet, I'm now confident enough to play in front of friends.

D   **Margaret:** I find that a good laugh helps me to cheer up and feel younger even if I have a few aches and pains. For that reason, I make it part of my routine to go to my social club at least once a week. I love meeting old friends, making new ones and having a good laugh over a cup of tea. I like to join in with a board game as well. Sometimes I amaze people with the long words I come out with! I also do word searches, and I tackle the crossword every morning in the newspaper – just the simple one, I don't have time for the long one. Due to my love of word games, I started to play puzzles on my phone last year. This has brought me closer to my daughter in Australia as we exchange our scores every day. I love that.

Which person:

explains that some forms of meditation are useful for exercising your brain?	43	
mentions that growing older doesn't mean you have to stop doing things that make you happy?	44	
says that staying sociable lifts your mood even if you're not feeling your best?	45	
says that activities keep you physically and mentally healthy and also help you maintain relationships?	46	
suggests that you should try to live in the moment every once in a while?	47	
thinks both mental and physical health need to be treated equally?	48	
likes to play games to stay connected to friends and family?	49	
believes that people can enjoy life by appreciating small moments of joy?	50	
states that it's possible and beneficial to find new hobbies later in life?	51	
thinks that getting rid of pessimistic influences can be necessary at times?	52	

Answer sheet   Test No. ☐

Mark out of 22 ☐

Name _____   Date _____

Part 5   *6 marks*

Mark the appropriate answer (A, B, C or D).

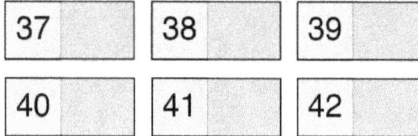

31	A B C D	34	A B C D
32	A B C D	35	A B C D
33	A B C D	36	A B C D

Part 6   *6 marks*

Add the appropriate answer (A–G).

| 37 | 38 | 39 |
| 40 | 41 | 42 |

Part 7   *10 marks*

Add the appropriate answer (A, B, C or D).

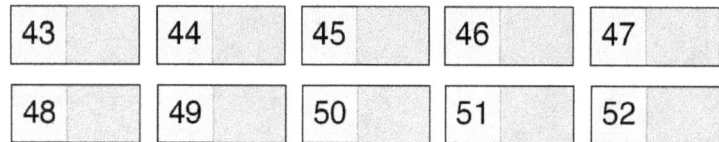

Cambridge B2 First Reading

Test 4

Cambridge B2 First Reading

Part 5

You are going to read an extract from an article about Supercentenarians – people who have reached the age of 100 years or more. For questions 31–36, read the text below and decide which answer fits best according to the text. In the separate answer sheet, mark the appropriate answer (A, B, C or D).

Supercentenarians are among the oldest and most remarkable individuals in the world. They represent a tiny amount of the global population, and only a small number of people ever make it to this incredible age. According to the Gerontology Research Group, there are currently around 30-to-40 confirmed supercentenarians worldwide. However, there may be a significantly higher number in reality, and numbers are growing with the increase in the length of time humans are now living.

Despite the advances in modern medicine, the reasons why some individuals manage to live past 110 years are generally unknown. Some research suggests that our ancestors and our biology play a role, with certain biological markers appearing to confer a degree of protection against age-related illnesses. Others suggest that lifestyle factors, such as diet, exercise and social support, may also contribute to living a long life.

All supercentenarians have witnessed some of the most significant events of the past century, and have lived through times of war and peace, and vast social, cultural and technological changes. One such supercentenarian, and one of the oldest, is Mrs Maisie Smith, who, at 112 years old, has lived through the 20th century and into the 21st century. I first caught up with Mrs Smith at her 112th birthday party, surrounded by her friends and descendants.

"The first time I saw an aeroplane fly, I was playing in the fields with some friends and we heard a funny noise. Then we saw the plane and we were lucky enough that it flew right overhead – amazing! There was only the pilot in the plane, but I think he saw us. I couldn't believe it. I had never seen anything like it before or even see a pilot. It was a wonderful experience. It must have been another 40 years before I got to go in one myself though."

Maisie lived through two World Wars, and they undoubtedly left their mark.

"It was tough. We had to make the best of things. I lost my brother in France in 1916, and my husband came home from the Second World War wounded so I was caring for him. That was a hard time for me with three young children in the house as well. There was a lot of uncertainty and poverty during those times, but I did what we had to do and we made it through."

And having witnessed so many changes over the years, what does Maisie think about the world today?

"People are always asking me that!" she says. "All the computers and everybody travelling around the world. You can do things in seconds that would have taken us years – I think it's wonderful. But I think it's getting harder to be old. My town has no bank or post office anymore. It seems that if you can't get onto a computer nobody cares about you. I'm glad to see progress being made in many areas, but why aren't people remembering that older people deserve respect and aren't all able to access things in the same way as young people are?"

And what advice does Maisie have for people who want to live as long as she has? "Keep working for as long as you can! I started work young – nobody cared so much about school or studying in those days, not like they do these days – and I kept going for years. Even when I retired, I worked hard in the garden and around the house. And I always have a little piece of chocolate every day – that gives me something to look forward to!"

31 According to the text, how do Supercentenarians live for such a long time?

   A The reasons still remain a mystery.
   B Because modern medicine has helped them to live longer.
   C The most significant factor is family history.
   D Because they have received more support than other generations.

32 In the first paragraph, the writer says that

   A there is an exact and correct number of supercentenarians on record.
   B there are many people who now make it to this milestone.
   C there are possibly more supercentenarians worldwide than we know about.
   D there are more supercentenarians now than there will be in future.

33 In the fourth paragraph, what does Maisie say about the plane?

   A She and her friends were afraid of the sound they heard.
   B She had to wait several decades before going on her first flight.
   C She felt the plane flew too close to where she was.
   D She decided she would like to meet a pilot.

34 Maisie lived through two world wars and says that

   A she tries not to think about the people she lost.
   B she would not have survived without the support of her family.
   C she felt lonely while her husband was fighting.
   D she was able to overcome the many difficulties.

35 What does Maisie say about modern life?

   A She thinks the disadvantages of modern life are more than the benefits.
   B She says that most older people aren't fans of technology.
   C She feels that there are not enough considerations for older people.
   D She suggests that younger people are impatient and do not respect older people.

36 What does Maisie think is the key to her long life?

   A work and small pleasures.
   B work and education.
   C education and small pleasures.
   D work and an active lifestyle.

Part 6

You are going to read an extract from a magazine article in which the writer reviews a live music gig. Six sentences have been removed. For questions 37–42, read the text below and, in the separate answer sheet, choose from options A–G the sentence that fits each gap. There is one extra sentence that you do not need to use.

Gig review

Frostfire at Wembley Stadium

Frostfire is one of the hottest pop stars around, and her recent tour showed why. Last night, fans lined up for miles around Wembley Stadium to see her perform, and it was clear from the start that it was going to be a night to remember.

The gig was the highlight of Frostfire's recent sell-out, 36-show tour. [37] Originally from New York, Frostfire – real name Amy Winters – could never have imagined that she would be stepping out into the spotlight from her humble beginnings. Only 18 months ago she was auditioning for a well-known TV show and was actually advised not to give up her day job by judge Eric Trowell. How wrong he has been proven.

[38] Amy took on the name Frostfire, and the rest, as they say, is history.

However, even Aristra Records must be surprised by the success of the first album 'Speechless'. It was at the top of the charts within four weeks, and sales have gone from strength to strength over the last 12 months. It was number 1 on the US Billboard Chart for 12 straight weeks at one point. In the original tour the largest venue booked had a capacity of 12,000. [39] As 90,000 people attended this arena, you could feel the excitement. The stage was set and the lights were dimmed. Suddenly, the place erupted in cheers as Frostfire appeared on stage, dressed in a stunning outfit that sparkled under the lights.

From the first note of the opening song, the crowd was inspired. [40] The energy in the room was incredible, with everyone on their feet, dancing to the music.

I was really impressed by the choreography throughout the show. Frostfire showed echoes of Madonna in her heyday, moving effortlessly around the stage with outstanding dancing.

The gig was packed with hit after hit, each with its own catchy and memorable lyrics, and Frostfire kept the crowd entertained throughout. [41] This perfectly created love song has been the most played song on every major music platform in recent months, and played live it was just as heart-breaking as the album version, even when performed just by Frostfire and her guitarist Titus Stevens. It's a firm fans' favourite too.

Another highlight was a cover song of Winston Branthorp's 1970's classic Over and Over. [42] The support bands were also fantastic, turning the concert into its own mini festival. Myles Brightman and the Showmen were absolutely phenomenal and entertained in the 40 minutes they had leading up to the main show.

In conclusion: nothing short of incredible. Frostfire put on an unforgettable show that left fans excited long after it was over.

A Fans sang along to every word, their voices combining to create an amazing atmosphere.

B After that initial appearance on TV, social media was in support of Amy, and she was soon signed by Aristra Records, who immediately introduced her to a songwriter and went on an ambitious promotional tour.

C If you missed the support bands, you'll be annoyed later when they become as famous as the main act.

D In fact, extra dates had to be added, and in some cases venues were changed on account of Frostfire's incredible success over the past year.

E There were some truly standout moments, such as when she performed an acoustic version of Wasted Time on guitar.

F Nevertheless, it was the world-famous Wembley stadium that would be the place for last night's final show of the tour.

G It is just as well really that she gets away with doing other people's songs, as Frostfire's career has been so short that she only has one album from which to choose songs for a concert.

Cambridge B2 First Reading

Part 7

You are going to read a newspaper article about animal migration – when animals move from one place to another. Six sentences have been removed. For questions 43–52, read the text below and, in the separate answer sheet, choose the correct paragraph (A–D).

Animal migration: Tracing the migration patterns of different animals

A The grey whale is known for its long annual migration between its summer feeding grounds in the Arctic and its winter breeding grounds in the warmer waters of Mexico. Grey whales typically begin their migration in the autumn, when they start to move south from their summer feeding grounds, passing through the waters of Alaska, Canada and the United States before arriving at their winter breeding grounds off the coast of Mexico. They follow a carefully chosen route, and tend to follow the coastline, which provides a familiar landmark. Along the way, they may stop to rest in sheltered bays or coves. The grey whale migration is not only a natural wonder but also a crucial part of the global ecosystem. As they move along their journey, grey whales stir up the bottom of the ocean floor, which helps to distribute nutrients and make new homes for other marine life.

B During the summer months, caribou can often be found at the top of hills in alpine meadows, where they feed on grasses and other plants. In the winter, they migrate to lower meadows and forests, where they feed on plants, mosses and shrubs. The migration patterns of caribou vary depending on the region and where they spend most of their time. Caribou migration is one of the most spectacular events in the animal kingdom, and one of the longest of any land mammal, with some travelling more than 2,500 miles each. Their migration journey is proof of their determination. As the weather warms up in the spring, the caribou begin their migration, walking thousands of miles across mountains and rivers. Along the way, they must pass through rough lands, avoid predators and search for food and water.

C The Chinook salmon, also known as king salmon, is a species of fish that is famous for its annual migration from the ocean to freshwater streams and rivers. Their migration begins when the adults set off from the ocean and swim upriver. They navigate their way upstream against strong currents, rapids and waterfalls, often jumping out of the water in a spectacular display. The journey can be long and tough, with some Chinook salmon traveling over 1,000 miles. On arrival, the females will typically dig a nest in the riverbed and lay their eggs, which are then covered with small stones to protect them from danger. After releasing their eggs, the Chinook salmon will typically die, as the physical demands of the journey is too great for them to survive for long. However, the eggs they have laid will eventually grow and the fish will make their way to the ocean.

D The migration of the monarch butterfly is a remarkable natural event that takes place every year across North America. It involves millions of butterflies travelling thousands of miles, from their breeding grounds in the United States and Canada all the way to where they stay for winter. The journey begins in late summer, when the adult monarchs come out of their cocoons and begin to feed on nectar to build up their energy for the long journey ahead. Once they are ready, they set off on their journey and to leave the colder climate, in search of warmer climates and better food sources. Once the monarchs arrive at their winter home, they come together in huge numbers to form close groups in the branches of trees. There, they will spend the winter months, saving their energy and waiting for the spring to arrive.

Which animals:

are at risk during their migration because of dangerous elements and landscapes? | 43

travel from north to south on their migration route? | 44

keep their future young safe by burying them? | 45

help create places to live for other species? | 46

usually use so much energy during their migration that they cannot live? | 47

make a vital contribution to the survival of other species? | 48

are not very active during the winter and use that time to rest? | 49

have different migration patterns among the species depending on the area in which they live? | 50

migrate based on a combination of temperature and food options? | 51

move to higher ground during the warmer months? | 52

Answer sheet   Test No. ☐

                                                  Mark out of 22 ☐

Name _____   **Date** _____

Part 5   *6 marks*

Mark the appropriate answer (A, B, C or D).

| 0 | A ☐ | B ☐ | C ■ | D ☐ |

31	A ☐	B ☐	C ☐	D ☐		34	A ☐	B ☐	C ☐	D ☐
32	A ☐	B ☐	C ☐	D ☐		35	A ☐	B ☐	C ☐	D ☐
33	A ☐	B ☐	C ☐	D ☐		36	A ☐	B ☐	C ☐	D ☐

Part 6   *6 marks*

Add the appropriate answer (A–G).

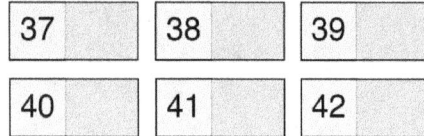

Part 7   *10 marks*

Add the appropriate answer (A, B, C or D).

| 43 | 44 | 45 | 46 | 47 |
| 48 | 49 | 50 | 51 | 52 |

Cambridge B2 First Reading

Test 5

Part 5

You are going to read an extract from a blog post written by a foreign language student. For questions 31–36, read the text below and decide which answer fits best according to the text. In the separate answer sheet, mark the appropriate answer (A, B, C or D).

As a foreign language student, I had to make a tough decision about where to study English. Studying English abroad can be an exciting and life-changing experience, but it is important to consider a few key factors before making the decision.

Firstly, you should research the country and culture you will be studying in, as this will help you to adjust to your new surroundings and make the most of your experience. There are many English-speaking countries to choose from, including the United States, Canada, Australia, and the United Kingdom. It is then important to consider the cost of living and the quality of education offered by language schools or universities. You can ensure that you make the most of your time abroad by taking these things into account.

Line 9

It was not an easy choice for me to make, but, after much consideration, I decided to choose Ireland. Something deep down just told me I was making the right choice. I knew that Ireland was a small island country with a rich culture and friendly people. I also knew that it was an English-speaking country, which meant that I would be surrounded by the language, which was what I wanted. I had heard mixed reviews about the country, with some people saying that the weather can be awful, but others had given great recommendations. The rain couldn't put me off, and I decided to trust my initial thoughts and feelings and choose Ireland as my destination.

When I arrived, nothing could have prepared me for just how stunning the country was. The rolling hills, green fields and coastline were breathtaking. The local people were welcoming and easy to talk to, and I felt like I had made the right choice. I was excited to start my English language studies. I signed up to an English language school in Dublin, and my first few days were a bit scary. Everything was new, and it was difficult to find my way around at first. However, I was determined to make the most of my experience. I made friends with international students from all over the world in the first few weeks and began to explore the small yet wonderful city.

My English language classes were challenging, but the teachers were amazing compared to those at home. For a start, they were kind and encouraging, and really pushed me to improve my language, even in a class size as large as 25 students. My grammar, vocabulary and pronunciation all improved dramatically. Overall, I was amazed at how much I learned in such a short period. In addition to my language classes, I also took part in cultural activities organised by the school such as Irish dancing, music and cuisine. I even had the opportunity to attend a traditional Irish wedding, which was an unforgettable experience.

One of the things that I loved about studying in Ireland was the opportunity to practise my English in real-world situations. Although acting things out in lessons was useful in preparing me for the outside world, I was grateful to use the language in actual, everyday situations, such as ordering food in a restaurant, buying groceries and chatting with locals. This helped me to become more confident in my language skills and it improved my fluency. I even started going to local pubs for conversation evenings, but that was more to socialise with my friends from school than anything else.

Overall, my experience of studying English in Ireland was incredible. The country, people and culture went above and beyond what I'd expected, and I made memories that will last a lifetime. I would highly recommend Ireland to anyone considering studying English as a foreign language. The quality of education, the friendly people and the beautiful scenery make it an ideal destination for language learners. And, despite the initial concerns about the weather, I found that the climate in Ireland was not as bad as I had expected.

31 'these' in line 9 refers to

  A the countries that have English as their native language.
  B the financial costs and education standards.
  C the types of educational institutions you can attend.
  D the challenges of adjusting to a new environment.

32 Which is true of the author's decision-making process?

  A She was unsure about being surrounded by English all the time.
  B She chose Ireland because of the entirely positive feedback from other people.
  C She considered not going to Ireland because of the bad weather.
  D She followed her feelings in order to make her choice.

33 What does the author say about her first few weeks in Ireland?

  A She did not expect to make friends so quickly.
  B She did not believe in her English language abilities.
  C She did not expect the city to be the size it was.
  D She did not know how beautiful it would be.

34 What were the author's thoughts about her lessons?

  A The activities organised by the school were unusual.
  B There were fewer students in the class than expected.
  C The teachers were better than teachers in her home country.
  D She would have liked to improve her pronunciation more.

35 The author was able to build her confidence with English by

  A interacting with local people outside the classroom.
  B practising the language with friends from the language centre.
  C acting out everyday situations in the classroom.
  D joining a conversation evening at a local pub.

36 What does the author think about her decision to study in Ireland?

  A The weather and the climate remained difficult to adjust to.
  B There were many things that were much better than she had imagined.
  C The country has the most beautiful scenery she has ever seen.
  D There were days when she improved her language more than others.

Part 6

You are going to read an extract from an article about the history of flying. Six sentences have been removed. For questions 37–42, read the text below and, in the separate answer sheet, choose from options A–G the sentence that fits each gap. There is one extra sentence that you do not need to use.

Transatlantic flights
Testing the limits of human ambition

The history of transatlantic aviation – flights that cross the Atlantic Ocean – is a story of human ambition; of taking risks and going beyond what was once considered impossible.

When the first transatlantic flights took off in the early 20th century, they represented not only a new way to travel but also a cultural revolution that would change the world forever.

In the early days of aviation, flying across the Atlantic was seen as a dangerous task that many experts thought was impossible. **37** In fact, history was made in 1919, when British pilots John Alcock and Arthur Whitten Brown flew nonstop from Newfoundland to Ireland in just over 16 hours, proving that transatlantic flight was indeed possible. Their flight was far from comfortable, however, as their plane was a First World War bomber, but their reward – £10,000 from a national newspaper – made it worthwhile.

Over the next few decades, aviation technology continued to change, with the introduction of the jet engine making long-distance flights more efficient and affordable. In 1958, the first transatlantic passenger jet service took off, with BOAC's Comet 4 flying from London to New York in just seven hours. **38** In the 1970s, supersonic flights were introduced – flights which travelled faster than the speed of sound – with the famous Concorde taking passengers from London to New York in just 3.5 hours. **39** For most people, faraway travel remained a luxury that was only affordable for the wealthy.

But over time the rise of economy class and low-cost airlines changed the game once again, making transatlantic travel more accessible than ever before. Today, millions of people queue up for transatlantic flights every year, with new technologies and innovations making the experience faster, more comfortable and more affordable than ever before.

40 One such area of focus and evolution is sustainability, with airlines and aircraft manufacturers investing in new technologies to reduce pollution and reduce the environmental impact of air travel. **41** Another option is electric or hybrid aircraft, which would rely on electric motors, for take-off and landing, and conventional engines for cruising. While these technologies are still in the early stages of development, they represent a significant step forward in creating a more sustainable future for air travel.

Looking back at the history of transatlantic aviation, it's hard to believe just how far we've come. Who would have believed that it would be possible to travel from Bangkok to Barcelona in a few hours? **42** Transatlantic aviation has changed the world in many ways, opening up new opportunities for trade, commerce and cultural exchange.

And as the technology continues to develop, who knows what the future of trans-atlantic travel will bring? One thing is for sure: the dream of flight will always be a part of our human experience, inspiring us to take off and explore the unknown.

A   The future of transatlantic flights is an exciting topic for discussion, with many potential developments on the horizon.

B   This marked a new era in transatlantic travel, as more and more people began to take for granted the ability to go up in an aeroplane and travel to distant lands.

C   One of the most promising developments in this regard is the use of fuels, which come from natural sources like algae and can reduce carbon emissions by up to 80%.

D   And yet, today we forget to appreciate that we can head off to a faraway destination such as these at a moment's notice.

E   But as the technology improved and pilots became more skilled, the dream of transatlantic flight started to become a reality.

F   This type of aircraft was a major breakthrough in aviation technology, but the high cost of these flights meant that they were only available to a chosen few.

G   From hot air balloons to today's possibilities for more sustainable air travel, transatlantic aviation certainly started from simple beginnings.

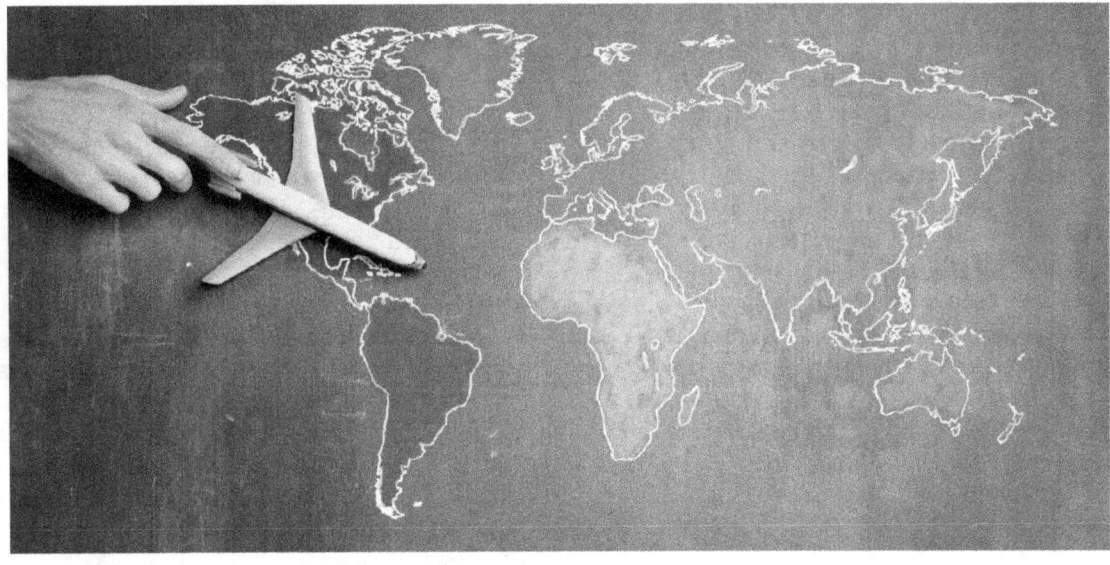

Part 7

You are going to read a newspaper article about people looking for rental accommodation in London. Six sentences have been removed. For questions 43–52, read the text below and, in the separate answer sheet, choose the correct paragraph (A–D).

Renting property in London

A **Simon:** After recently splitting up with my partner, I'm eager to move out of our shared flat and find a place to myself. It's important to me to have my own space where I can feel comfortable and independent. However, I don't have much of a budget to work with, so finding a suitable flat has been a bit of a challenge. All I want is a cosy space that feels like home – without breaking the bank. At the same time, I'm being careful not to compromise on the quality of the flat, as I want to make sure it's a place where I can truly be happy. It's a bit scary to think about, but I'm excited to see what the future will bring and to find the perfect flat that I can call my own.

B **Marco:** I just need to get out of my current situation. I've been living in a shared flat for the past year, and, while it's been fun, it's time for a change. I've been looking into different options, and I think a small studio flat would do just fine. I don't need much space – that's not important for me – just somewhere I can call my own and have a bit of privacy. One thing that is essential for me when it comes to finding a new flat is parking. I have a car, and it's important to me that I can park it nearby without any worries. I'm also quite particular about being clean, so a flat where everyone takes care of their own washing up would be important to me. I'm generally very relaxed and get on well with most people, so I'm hoping to find some friendly and respectful housemates. Living in a place where I can relax and feel at home is very important to me.

C **David:** I'm currently hunting for a house to rent as I'm hoping to move in with my three teenage daughters, so having a bit more space is crucial. I don't have much time as we need to move in the next few months, so I've been busy making arrangements and viewing properties. Ideally, we need a house with four bedrooms, so that everyone can have a room of their own and we can hopefully avoid any arguments and not annoy each other. Additionally, it's important to me that the house has good public transport links, as I rely on public trans-port to get to work. I've been looking into different areas and checking the transport routes, as I don't want to end up in a place that's too difficult to get to. I'm hopeful that we'll find the perfect house soon, and that we can all settle in and make it a happy home.

D **Imran:** I've been looking for a new house to rent for me and my family. We're currently in a small flat, and we're in desperate need of more space. I'd been looking at different properties online, but I decided to take a more active approach and asked around to see if anyone knew of any houses available to rent. Luckily, a friend of a friend had recently moved out of their house and into a new place, leaving the property vacant. I arranged to go and take a look at the house, and it seemed like the perfect fit for us. The only concern I had was whether or not the landlord would approve us to live there. I wasn't sure if my rental history was strong enough, so I asked a friend who works as an estate agent to speak on my behalf. Finally, after a few anxious days, we received confirmation that we had been approved to rent the house. At the very least, the house has two bedrooms, one for my wife and me, and one for our two young children who will share a room. Plus there's even parking for both of our cars, which is a huge bonus. We're excited to move it and make it our own.

Which person:

believes that the size of a property is not really a priority?	43
thinks that living with messy people would be less than ideal?	44
suggests that finding a way to avoid getting on each other's nerves is a priority?	45
says that he might not be able to afford the right property?	46
thinks that easy access to the property is a key factor?	47
describes how he had to change how he his originally searched?	48
explains that they are in a hurry to find somewhere?	49
says that he wants to find a new place because of a change in his relationship?	50
mentions that his social connections have been beneficial?	51
explains that car parking is a vital element of his search?	52

Answer sheet Test No. ☐

Mark out of 22 ☐

Name _____ Date _____

Part 5 *6 marks*

Mark the appropriate answer (A, B, C or D).

31	A B C D		34	A B C D
32	A B C D		35	A B C D
33	A B C D		36	A B C D

Part 6 *6 marks*

Add the appropriate answer (A–G).

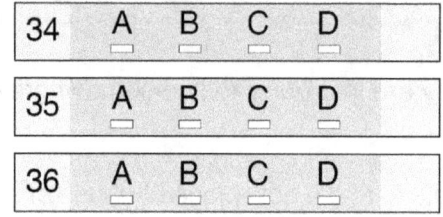

Part 7 *10 marks*

Add the appropriate answer (A, B, C or D).

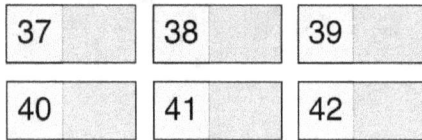

Cambridge B2 First Reading

Test 6

Cambridge B2 First Reading

Part 5

You are going to read an extract from a blog in which a woman describes clearing out her grandmother's attic. For questions 31–36, read the text below and decide which answer fits best according to the text. In the separate answer sheet, mark the appropriate answer (A, B, C or D).

As I began to clear out my grandmother's attic, I couldn't believe how much stuff had gathered over the years – amazing things that I had enjoyed and loved throughout my childhood. Doing this felt like a hugely stressful job, but I was determined to see it through. As the only grandchild I felt it was my responsibility. I began by sorting things into piles: things to keep, things to throw out and things to donate.

Believe me, the pile of things to throw out looked almost like a mountain by the time I'd finished, and I was tempted just to throw everything away. But my mother suggested that I donate as much as I could – unless there was anything I wanted to keep – and I eventually agreed with her. In the end, there was almost nothing to throw out! I've put everything into my mum's car to prepare for the many trips to charity shops and the recycling centre that we have to make in the next few weeks.

However, it wasn't all bad news. As I sorted through boxes of familiar family photos, 1960s clothes and bags of old toys my mum used to play with when she was younger, I came across a dusty old wooden box that I had never seen before. I wiped away the cobwebs and lifted the lid, unsure of what I would find inside. To my surprise, I discovered an antique treasure – a beautiful, handmade wooden jewellery box. The complicated details and craftsmanship were breathtaking, and I couldn't believe it had been hidden away for so long. I have no idea who it belonged to originally, but I'm planning to take it to an antique shop to have it valued. Who knows? It might be an incredibly valuable treasure.

Even more importantly, after the excitement of finding the jewellery box, I found a pile of old letters hidden behind my grandfather's old armchair. These documents had been passed down through generations of my family. As I read through the letters and looked through the photos among the letters, I felt like I was taking a trip into the past. I saw pictures of my grandparents when they were young, read letters written by my great-grandparents when they were first going out together, and I learned about family members that I had never met. I knew that these items were too precious to throw out or donate to a charity shop, but I did think they might be useful for a local history display. Unfortunately, there aren't any local museums near my grandmother's house. So instead, after showing them to my mother, I carefully put them back into the box and made a mental note to preserve them for my children and my grandchildren.

As I continued to clear out the attic, I came across other items that were very special. I found old drawings and books from my childhood, as well as things that had been passed down to me from my parents and grandparents. One very special find was a notebook full of signatures from pop stars from the 1970s and 80s that must have been collected by my mother when she was a teenager. I took them round to her when I visited last week, and she was over the moon to see them as she had thought that her parents must have thrown them out when she left home. I knew that these items would be important to my own children someday, so I will make sure that I hand them over to my kids with care.

Tidying out the attic ended up being much more than just cleaning out old things – it was a journey of discovery and a chance to reconnect with my family's past. I was grateful for the opportunity to find these hidden treasures, and I knew that they would be appreciated for years to come.

31 What was the author's attitude to clearing the attic?

    A She really enjoyed the process.

    B She felt the pressure of the task at hand.

    C She wanted to quit halfway through.

    D she wished that she had received help from her sister.

32 In paragraph 2, what does the author say she needs to do in the near future?

    A Take her grandmother's things to various places.

    B Throw her grandmother's belongings away.

    C Discuss with her mum what to do with her grandmother's things.

    D Go through her grandmother's things to decide what to keep for herself.

33 What did the author find that was particularly interesting?

    A family pictures she had never seen before

    B several valuable antiques

    C toys which had been played with for generations

    D a beautiful and mysterious box

34 What does the author do with the pictures and the letters?

    A She gives them to her mother.

    B She takes them to a shop that accepts donations.

    C She takes them to a local history museum.

    D She decides to keep them for future generations.

35 What other items carry important memories for the author?

    A Her mother's old pictures and books.

    B Items her grandparents had given her parents.

    C A book the author kept about famous people.

    D Things her grandparents wanted her to give her own children.

36 In the final paragraph, the author says that

    A she was lucky to have discovered the special objects.

    B she can now give more information about her past to her own family.

    C she would like to connect more with her past.

    D she found some secret objects she will keep from her parents.

Part 6

You are going to read an extract from magazine article that talks about light festivals. Six sentences have been removed. For questions 37–42, read the text below and, in the separate answer sheet, choose from options A–G the sentence that fits each gap. There is one extra sentence that you do not need to use.

Festivals of light

Mixing old traditions with new to celebrate light

Festivals of light are a celebration of human creativity. [37] Today, festivals that use lights are celebrated worldwide and bring together people from all walks of life to look at the beauty of light displays.

One of the most famous light festivals is Christmas, which is celebrated in many countries worldwide. [38] These days, Christmas lights are a crucial part of the holiday season, with many cities and towns around the world decorating their streets with huge displays.

Another well-known light festival is Diwali, which is celebrated in India and other countries with large Hindu populations. [39] Diwali is also known for its spectacular firework displays, which are meant to protect you from evil spirits and welcome success and happiness.

The Lantern Festival is a Chinese festival celebrated on the 15th day of the first lunar month, which usually happens in February or March. During the festival, people light and release paper bags lit with candles into the sky to symbolise the release of worries and troubles. [40]

While these festivals have historical and cultural significance, they can also come with a significant cost. In some cases, cities and towns spend millions of dollars on detailed lighting systems and decorations. [41] However, despite the cost, festivals that use lights continue to draw large crowds of people who are eager to witness the spectacle of illuminated displays. In recent years, many festivals have become more tech-savvy, incorporating cutting-edge technologies like LEDs and interactive displays. The latest fashion is for drone shows that create amazing 3D shapes in the air. These advances in technology have made such festivals even more breathtaking and engaging, with displays that are in a class of their own.

Festivals that use lights are a celebration of human creativity and design. [42] Whether it is Christmas or Diwali, these festivals have a rich historical and cultural context that continues to inspire people worldwide. Therefore, festivals that use lights must balance the desire for spectacle with the need for sustainability and the responsible use of resources.

A After they have flown into the air, the festival, which has its roots in Buddhism and Taoism, then continues with lion dances and fireworks.

B The origins of the festival date back to ancient celebrations of the winter solstice, which were celebrated with the lighting of fires and candles.

C While they can come at a high cost, they bring together people from all walks of life to see the beauty of the light displays.

D From ancient religious festivals to modern-day parties, light has played an important role in human cultures throughout history.

E Many cities worldwide even host these types of festivals to see which street or neighbourhood has the most beautiful or even extreme Christmas lights, attracting people in their hundreds.

F This festival is celebrated across much of the country, and marks the lighting of lamps and candles.

G While these displays can be amazing, it is important not to go too far for beauty or entertainment.

Part 7

You are going to read a newspaper article about the challenges and rewards of giving up technology. Six sentences have been removed. For questions 43–52, read the text below and, in the separate answer sheet, choose the correct paragraph (A–D).

Digital detox
Four people describe the challenges and rewards of giving up technology

A **Shahanna:** As someone who has always been addicted to internet games, deciding to give up all digital devices for a week was a challenge. Without my usual distractions, I found myself with a lot of free time, and I didn't know what to do with it. I wouldn't say I was bored, but I definitely felt uncomfortable. I tried to make the best of things and found alternative ways to spend my time. I picked up a new hobby, started reading more books and spent more time with family and friends. In contrast to my usual routine, I felt more in the moment, and my relationships with others improved. After that week, I realised that I had been using gaming to avoid being bored and had been missing out on so much of what life has to offer.

B **Peter:** I was a teenager before mobiles and devices took off, but like everyone else these days I'm used to being stuck to my mobile 24–7. I recently decided to switch off from all digital devices for a week. Once I got used to it I found it really easy to relax without any interruptions. During the digital detox, I realised how much time I had wasted on social media. Instead, I played my guitar for the first time in months, which I'd really missed doing, and read some of my favourite books. Even though I was tempted to check my phone a few times or message my brother, I resisted the urge and enjoyed the peace and quiet. Then, I began to realise that people need to use their imagination more, play games and sometimes just relax in peace and quiet.

C **Giuliana:** At first, it was a bit of a shock, and I found myself wanting to look at my phone to check messages and social media. But after a while I began to relax and take pleasure in the simple things in life without constant interruptions. However, as the days went by, I found that my dependence on technology had been impacting my ability to sleep. Without my usual routines, I couldn't sleep at night and found myself passing out in the middle of the day. I also got really bored and had to find new ways to occupy my time. Actually, I discovered that my usual tech-based hobbies had been keeping me stressed out and anxious, and that taking a break from them was good for me. I think that we are over-dependent on technology, and it is important to go to extremes sometimes to find a healthy balance in life.

D Judith: I wanted to take a fresh start to reset my mind and limit my screen time. At first, it was difficult to put off the need to keep on checking my phone or social media, but as time went on I felt more at ease and present in the moment. However, during this digital detox, I noticed that my sister was struggling to put her phone down. I had not realised how dependent she had become on technology until then. I tried to make her see reason, and I encouraged her to take a break, but she was resistant. I hope that my experience can serve as an example to others in a similar situation, as we all need to disconnect from time to time and appreciate the world around us without distractions.

Which person:

says that they didn't have a lot of technology in their early childhood?	43
mentions that they felt that their human connections benefited from the digital break?	44
hopes that they can inspire others who might be addicted to technology?	45
was able to spend more time on a hobby they hadn't done recently?	46
suggests that taking action such as a digital break is necessary at times?	47
states that their main digital occupation had been playing different online games?	48
explains that technology had been responsible for their anxiety?	49
is concerned about someone else's use of technology?	50
thinks that their technology use affected their physical health?	51
explains that they decided to try a new activity with their extra time?	52

Answer sheet   Test No. ☐

Mark out of 22 ☐

Name _____   Date _____

Part 5   *6 marks*

Mark the appropriate answer (A, B, C or D).

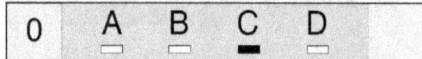

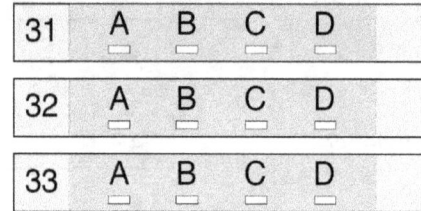 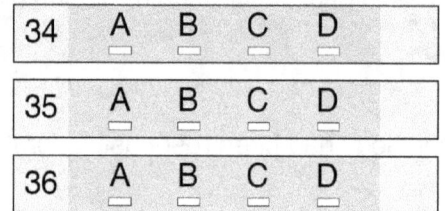

Part 6   *6 marks*

Add the appropriate answer (A–G).

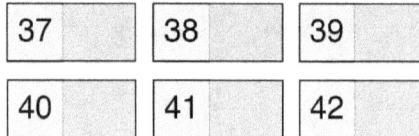

Part 7   *10 marks*

Add the appropriate answer (A, B, C or D).

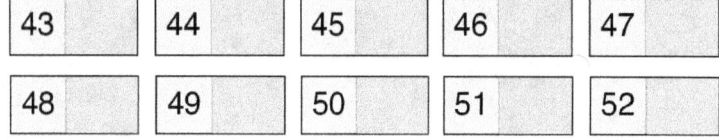

Cambridge B2 First Reading

Test 7

Cambridge B2 First Reading

Part 5

You are going to read an extract from a blog post in which a sleep therapist – someone who helps people to sleep better – talks about her work. For questions 31–36, read the text below and decide which answer fits best according to the text. In the separate answer sheet, mark the appropriate answer (A, B, C or D).

As a sleep therapist, my daily tasks involve helping people get off to sleep and wake up feeling good. It's a job that I'm passionate about, as I know first-hand the impact that sleep can have on a person's overall health and well-being. As a teenager I struggled with insomnia, which meant I couldn't sleep, and it had a significant impact on my daily life. I found myself unable to fall asleep despite feeling exhausted. When I did finally manage to sleep, I often woke up multiple times throughout the night, leaving me feeling horrible the next day. My insomnia was particularly frustrating because I felt like I was doing everything 'right' in terms of my sleep habits. I went to bed at the same time each night, avoided coffee in the evening and created a relaxing bedtime routine. My mother even took me to see a sleep therapist. But despite my best efforts, I still couldn't sleep.

While my experience with insomnia was horrible, it ultimately taught me the importance of prioritising good sleep and seeking help when needed.

People often ask me how I got from there to becoming a sleep therapist myself. My educational background is in psychology. After completing my degree, I went on to study therapy – a one-year course during which I gained experience working with clients who were struggling with sleep-related issues. Throughout my studies, I took courses that focused on sleep issues, and I also did a lot of hands-on work advising clients with these problems. Even after completing my formal education, I carried on studying.

Line 17

Each day I work with clients to identify the causes of their sleep problems and develop plans personal to them, to improve the quality of their sleep. Some believe it's because they're not active enough during the day, while others believe it may be diet related. A few of my clients struggle to fall asleep at night so they turn to sleeping pills, which I wouldn't advise. Others find it difficult to stay asleep or wake up feeling rested. Through a combination of therapy and lifestyle changes, I help my clients to discover the causes of their sleep problems and establish healthy habits.

In addition to my work with clients, I also lead group sessions on topics like 'sleep hygiene', 'relaxation techniques' and 'stress management'. These sessions allow me to reach more people and provide them with the tools they need to improve their sleep quality and overall well-being.

One of the biggest issues these days is clients using their phones in the few hours before bed. Using mobile phones in the hours leading up to bedtime can damage sleep in several ways. The blue light which comes from electronic devices is just one of the factors that can make it more difficult to fall asleep and can also lead to poorer quality sleep overall. On top of the blue light, using mobile phones before bed can also make it harder to relax before sleep. Checking emails, looking through social media or responding to text messages can all awaken the brain, making it harder to get off to sleep.

Overall, to promote restful sleep it's best to avoid using mobile phones at night. The same is true for particularly hard exercise. A lot of people say listening to programmes about sleep or even drinking a hot, milky drink helps. I think the solutions are simpler than that. Instead, doing stress-free activities like reading a book, taking a warm bath or meditating can help prepare the body for sleep and improve the quality of rest throughout the night.

31 When describing her own sleep history, the therapist says that

  A she understands the problem due to her own sleep issues growing up.

  B she included a routine into her evenings to help with sleep.

  C she felt easily annoyed after a bad night's sleep.

  D she knew her mum was having difficulties sleeping that affected her.

32 How did the author become a sleep therapist?

  A She worked as a psychologist then switched to sleep therapy.

  B She got a university degree in sleep therapy.

  C She learned from therapists who were trained in sleep problems.

  D She did further training after her initial degree.

33 In line 17, 'hands-on work' means

  A doing manual tasks.

  B giving physical therapy.

  C working directly with people.

  D doing research using a variety of resources.

34 How does the therapist help people get better sleep?

  A She recommends medication to help people fall asleep.

  B She creates plans specific to each individual client.

  C She suggests that her clients get more regular exercise.

  D She comes up with meal plans to establish healthier habits.

35 What does the therapist say about using your phone before bed?

  A Using your phone for a few hours before sleeping is better than using it in bed.

  B The things people do on their phones make it difficult for their brains to rest.

  C Reading news or emails late at night can cause stress.

  D The phones' blue light is the main reason why people can't fall asleep.

36 What does the therapist recommend for a good night's sleep?

  A Do a heavy workout.

  B Listen to a radio show about sleep.

  C Do something relaxing.

  D Drink a hot chocolate or tea.

Part 6

You are going to read an extract from an article about a new sport introduced at the 2020 Tokyo Olympics. Six sentences have been removed. For questions 37–42, read the text below and, in the separate answer sheet, choose from options A–G the sentence that fits each gap. There is one extra sentence that you do not need to use.

Skateboarding at the 2020 Olympic Games
The style and skill of this new Olympic sport

Skateboarding was first at the 2020 Olympic Games in Tokyo (held in 2021), which was an extremely important moment for the sport. **37** This made the sport more engaging and interesting for many locals in the host country.

Skateboarding has long been regarded as an underground sport with its own subculture, often associated with people doing what they want and expressing themselves how they want. **38** Added to the feelings in the sport's community, the sport's high injury rate meant the Olympic committee was cautious about considering including it.

So, to finally see skateboarders at the Olympics was a huge achievement: putting the sport in the global spotlight, bringing it to a wider audience and giving skaters the recognition they deserve.

The sport's ability to appeal to both committed fans and new fans is evidence of its universal appeal. Jagger Eaton, an American bronze medallist, has said: "Skateboarding is an art form, and every one of us does it differently. Name another sport like that in the Olympic Games."

In contrast to the high levels of organization and discipline of more traditional Olympic events, skateboarding's informal and relaxed atmosphere creates a sense of family amongst the skaters. **39** This sense of community is particularly evident in the skate park, where skaters often help each other with tricks and encourage each other to push their limits.

Skateboarders at the Olympic Games compete in two disciplines: street and park. Each discipline features a variety of tricks that are judged based on factors such as difficulty, style and execution.

In the street discipline, skateboarders perform tricks on a course that recreates a real-world street environment. **40**

In the park discipline, skateboarders perform tricks on a bowl-shaped course that features a variety of transitions, curves and heights.

Despite facing challenges such as the need to hurry up and finish their run within a specific time or facing up to the fear of attempting difficult tricks in front of a large audience, skateboarders show a remarkable ability to get over such things and perform at their best. **41** They often came up with new tricks and combinations of tricks that were both difficult and visually stunning. Watching a skater land a trick perfectly is a wonderful thing.

Another thing that makes skateboarding different from other Olympic events is that each skater has their own style. **42** This makes for a more exciting and dynamic competition, as each skater's approach to the skate park is unique. The creativity on display in skateboarding is what makes it such an exciting sport to watch, and it's the reason why it has gained a devoted fanbase around the world. Even the judges at the Olympics award points for creativity.

The addition of skateboarding to the Olympics is a great opportunity for new generations of skaters to show their talents and inspire others. It will be exciting to see where the sport goes from here.

A   Skaters support each other, even if they are competing against each other, which is a nice change from other competitive sports.

B   Skateboarders at the 2020 Olympic Games showed themselves capable of pushing the limits of what is possible on a skateboard.

C   The host country dominated the medals, with three of the four golds going to Japanese skateboarders.

D   It was wonderful to see some of the legends of the skateboarding community, including Tony Hawk and Daewon Song, in the audience during the competition.

E   Skaters are encouraged to express themselves and show their individual personalities, which is why every skateboarder brings something different to the sport.

F   In fact, many of the sport's highest performers thought that the Olympics was not the right place for skateboarding.

G   This can include stairs, walls, slides and other objects and places.

Part 7

You are going to read a newspaper article about vinyl record collectors. Six sentences have been removed. For questions 43–52, read the text below and, in the separate answer sheet, choose the correct paragraph (A–D).

Vinyl records

Four collectors talk about their hobby

A Andrea: As a DJ, I'm always looking for the newest and most cutting-edge vinyl record releases to add to my collection. There's nothing quite like the feeling of walking into a record store and picking up a fresh vinyl, ready to play at my next concert. The sound quality of vinyl is incredible, and there's something special about hearing banging beats and catchy hooks on an old vinyl. From time to time, I'll come across a classic or rare album that I just can't resist adding to my collection. But, for the most part, I stick to new releases and new artists, always searching for the next big thing. There's something exciting about being ahead of the music trends and knowing what's cool in the industry. And, for me, there's no better way to experience music than on the warm, vintage sound of a vinyl record. It's not just about the music that comes through!

B Stuart: As the owner of a record shop, I need to keep up to date with the latest news on the music scene. But, for me, collecting vinyl records isn't just a business – it's a passion. I love being able to mix business with pleasure by stocking the shop with the latest releases for people to buy, while also adding to my own personal collection. While I do love picking up new albums, there's something special about hunting for second-hand treasures in thrift stores and estate sales. I love dealing with other people who are as enthusiastic as me, and it's a thrill to come across a rare album that I've been searching for, and my personal collection has grown to over 10,000 records as a result. Collecting vinyl has become a serious hobby for me, and I've even had to build an extension onto my house to store all of my wonderful albums.

C Kevin: I've been collecting vinyl records for over a decade now, and my collection has grown to over 1,000 records. I've always loved vintage records, particularly Northern Soul and Motown records from the 1960s and 1970s. It's been a passion of mine to build up my collection with these rare records, searching record stores and online marketplaces for any amazing pieces that I can get my hands on. For me, it's not just about the music: it's also about the records themselves. I love the artwork and I'm a real geek about the information provided. I really enjoy spotting who played guitar on the record and realizing that that person also played on another favourite album. You don't get that from a streaming service like Spotify. The tactile experience of holding a record makes all the difference to me. I'll always go for a record over a digital download – there's no comparison in my opinion.

D Donna: I may be new to record collecting, but I've quickly learned that it's not just about the music – it's also about the artwork on the vinyl record covers. I've spent hours browsing through second-hand record shops, searching for the most eye-catching designs. Of course, the condition of the record itself is important too, but I don't mind if it's a bit scratched or in bad shape as long as the artwork is still in good condition. I've notice that people often admire my collection, and it's great to be able to share my love for both the music and the artwork with others. I may not have the most expensive or rare records, but I've built up a collection that I'm proud of, and that's what really matters to me.

Which person:

is in the business of buying and selling records? | 43 |

says that seeing which musicians played on certain albums is interesting to them? | 44 |

describes how they had to create more space to store their records? | 45 |

explains that they've only recently started collecting vinyl records? | 46 |

says that they're always looking for new music on vinyl records to play at work? | 47 |

thinks that vinyl is much better than other music platforms or services? | 48 |

says they're into vinyl for both professional and personal reasons? | 49 |

mentions that the art and design of an album is what they're initially drawn to? | 50 |

thinks that they have a good-sized collection after several years? | 51 |

finds the sounds records make, aside from the music, to be very appealing? | 52 |

Answer sheet

Test No. ☐

Mark out of 22 ☐

Name _____   Date _____

Part 5 *6 marks*

Mark the appropriate answer (A, B, C or D).

| 0 | A ☐ B ☐ C ▬ D ☐ |

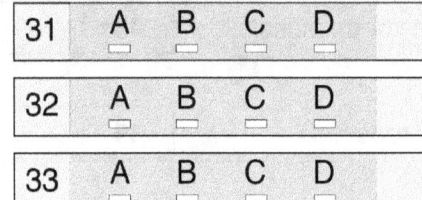   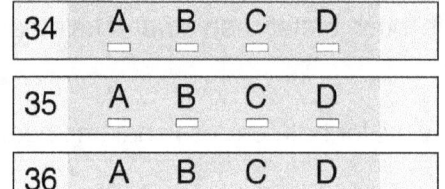

Part 6 *6 marks*

Add the appropriate answer (A–G).

| 37 | 38 | 39 |
| 40 | 41 | 42 |

Part 7 *10 marks*

Add the appropriate answer (A, B, C or D).

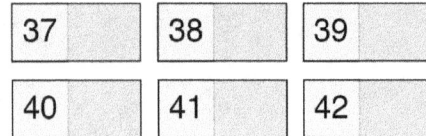

Cambridge B2 First Reading

Test 8

Cambridge B2 First Reading

Part 5

You are going to read an extract from a blog written by a postman. For questions 31–36, read the text below and decide which answer fits best according to the text. In the separate answer sheet, mark the appropriate answer (A, B, C or D).

As a postman, I deliver to a handful of islands around Scotland, each with its own unique character and challenges. Some are inhabited by just a few-dozen people, while others have larger populations and require more frequent deliveries. I've been fortunate enough to experience the beauty of these remote communities firsthand.

Delivering letters runs in the family. Growing up, I was surrounded by the hustle and bustle of my grandparents' village post office. My mother and her brothers and sisters were in charge of sorting the mail and handling customers, while my father was out delivering papers, letters and parcels to people's homes. I was always fascinated by the piles of letters, the stamps and the specific sorting system. I would even help out occasionally by sticking stamps on envelopes or packing parcels. It was no surprise to anyone when I decided to follow my father and take up a job as a postman. It was during the busy Christmas season when I first started, taking up a temporary job to help with the extra volume of mail. But once the holiday season was over, I found myself enjoying the job so much that I decided to stick around. Soon after beginning, I found myself delivering mail and supplies to the islands around Scotland, braving the rough seas and unpredictable weather. It was tough work, but I loved it.

Back then, the postal service in Scotland was very different from what it is now. We relied on boats to deliver mail to the islands, and the job required a lot of physical work. We had to lift heavy packages, travel across rough waters and be cautious when the weather turned bad. I remember one terrifying day when a storm came out of nowhere and, to make matters worse, our radio stopped working. Somehow we made it into port, and I have to admit that I still wake up in a cold sweat sometimes thinking about that trip. Even once we were on land, many of the roads were uneven and poorly maintained, and we had to carry out deliveries on foot in some cases, at Line 23 all hours of the day. But despite the challenges and heavy work, I made light work of it, and I soon began to take on more responsibilities.

As the years went by, the postal service in Scotland began to change. We started using helicopters and planes to deliver mail, which might sound a bit scary but reduced the number of challenges we faced. But even with these new technologies, we go above and beyond to ensure that our customers receive their mail on time. We still have to face the awful weather and deliver parcels to remote areas, but we always put our customers first.

Throughout my 40-year career, I have seen a lot of changes in the postal service. From changes in income to the methods for delivering the mail and even changes in the seasons, there have been very few things that have remained the same. But one thing that has never changed is the pleasure I get from delivering mail to the people of Scotland. It is a job that gives me a sense of purpose, and I'm proud to do it.

Nowadays, the postal service in Scotland is more efficient than ever before. We have new technologies and systems in place that make our jobs easier, but the commitment to customer service remains the same. During the Covid-19 pandemic, we played a vital role in delivering different things, such as medical supplies, letters to improve people's moods and online purchases to people during the lockdowns.

Whether you're delivering mail or working at the post office, it takes a committed team to keep the postal service running smoothly. And I'm so pleased to have been a part of that team for all these years.

31 What does the author say about the area where he works?

   A He lived in the areas he works.

   B He never sees many people.

   C He works mainly near Scotland's coastline.

   D He is surprisingly busy given the low population.

32 Why does the author say he decided to work as a postman?

   A He spent time going out with his father delivering mail.

   B He sorted the piles of mail that arrived at the post office.

   C He enjoyed interacting with customers who came to the post office.

   D He decided to do what his family members did.

33 The author describes how the postal service in Scotland has changed, and says that

   A the job used to be more physical.

   B there used to be less responsibility.

   C the methods of communication never used to work.

   D there used to be no roads to make deliveries.

34 In line 23, 'made light work of it' means

   A he agreed to take on less work.

   B he became more efficient at his job.

   C he worked during daytime hours.

   D he found the mail became easy to lift.

35 What impact did technology have on his work?

   A It led to a less personal relationship with customers.

   B It made certain parts of his job more dangerous.

   C It made aspects of his job much easier.

   D It made the weather less challenging.

36 What is the reason for the postman's job satisfaction?

   A feeling as though he is doing something meaningful.

   B the people he meets when he delivers.

   C seeing his team provide excellent customer service.

   D the speed at which things change in the industry.

Part 6

You are going to read a restaurant review. Six sentences have been removed. For questions 37–42, read the text below and, in the separate answer sheet, choose from options A–G the sentence that fits each gap. There is one extra sentence that you do not need to use.

Restaurant review: The Italian Kitchen

Highs but mostly lows at the newest Italian restaurant

The Italian Kitchen, just another small restaurant in a slightly out-of-the-way location, launched quietly last year, and I was fortunate to have been invited to the opening night to try the new menu of Italian pastas and pizzas. **37** The mysterious owner, Signor Rossi, had just gone out and never seemed to be around to talk to customers.

TV viewers of course will be familiar with this story. The Italian Kitchen was being secretly filmed from opening night, and the mysterious chef was none other than celebrity Tuscan chef Luca Rossi. Over ten episodes we have all been addicted to watching our screens, looking at the ups and downs of the restaurant's fortunes. Now of course, Luca Rossi has opened a chain of Italian Kitchens all over the UK, and I luckily managed to get myself and a friend tickets for the opening evening in Liverpool. **38** Despite being excited to try it out, I was disappointed from the moment I arrived.

First of all, the queue to get in was incredibly long, which is never a good sign. Once I finally got inside, I quickly realised that they had already run out of several menu items. Adding to this, we had to wait more than 30 minutes for our drinks to arrive, and we also noticed that some tables were being served before others, leaving some diners waiting while others had already finished their meals.

39 The walls were painted a horrible shade of red and the furniture looked like it had been quickly put together. It didn't create the cosy, warm atmosphere that I associate with Italian restaurants.

The food was the biggest let down of all. I ordered a pasta dish – a simple Fusilli alla Montanara – that was so disgusting that I had to hand it back to the server. **40** I was expecting real Italian cuisine, but what I got was not that.

To make matters worse, the service was incredibly poor. **41** When I tried to get her attention so that I could order a drink, she looked annoyed and took her time getting back to me.

Now, we do have to give credit where credit is due – the dessert certainly made up for it. The tiramisu was delicious and truly lived up to its reputation as a classic Italian dessert. It felt light and fluffy in my mouth, and had a lovely balance of sweetness and bitterness from the espresso and cocoa. It had been perfectly cooled before serving to help the flavours melt together and create a truly satisfying dessert. However, one good dish does not make up for the rest of the meal, which we didn't end up paying for as it was included in our high-ticket price.

I can't help but wonder where things went wrong. Was it the quality of the ingredients? The lack of attention to detail in the cooking? Or simply a bad day for the kitchen staff? **42**

Overall, I would give this restaurant a low star rating. It was a huge disappointment in every aspect. The food was not enjoyable, the service was poor and the atmosphere was miserable. Enough said.

A The pasta was overcooked, and the sauce tasted like it had come out of a can

B When the check finally came, I was not pleased to see the high price tag – who knew disappointment could cost so much?

C My server seemed uninterested in my table, and rarely checked on us throughout the meal.

D Expectations for the night were high, but I have to say that my experience was a huge let down.

E Whatever the cause, I have to advise you to look elsewhere for a quality Italian dining experience.

F The food was good, but anybody asking to meet the chef was disappointed.

G As I looked around the restaurant, the decoration made me uneasy.

Part 7

You are going to read a newspaper article about new music albums that readers have recommended. Six sentences have been removed. For questions 43–52, read the text below and, in the separate answer sheet, choose the correct paragraph (A–D).

This week's albums
Four albums recommended by readers

A **'2U' by Ava Lee:** Ava Lee's first-ever album '2U' is the hottest record of the year so far. The 18- year-old pop star has managed to get to number one with her first single 'In the Night' and her following hits 'Shy' and 'Shining Bright'. Her lyrics come from the heart and everyone can relate, which has helped her gain a massive following among teenagers. '2U' is a real earworm, with catchy hooks and memorable sounds. Despite the fact that some of her tracks deal with break ups and insecurity, Ava manages to make the overall sound of the album fun, fast-paced and has songs you'll remember. Above all, she has managed to create her own unique style, which is both refreshing and exciting.

B **'Midnight Voices' by Maxim and the Lost Toys:** Lost Toys' second album 'Midnight Voices' is a departure from their previous work. In contrast to the dark and moody tracks on their first album, 'Poppies', this album shows a more mature side of the UK's latest rock sensation. After the massive success of their debut, the Toys could have easily put out more of the same, but instead they chose to not listen to the outside noise and face up to their own feelings. The result is an album that is honest, raw and deeply personal. The instrumentation on the album is more basic and understated than on their previous work, allowing the focus to be on singer Maxim's voice and lyrics. Fans will respect this new direction. They will also likely find themselves listening to this album on repeat.

C **'Planet XY' by Luna Rae:** Luna Rae's third studio album 'Planet XY' is evidence of the artist's ability. The album does not sit in one category, as it shows Rae's many different influences, from pop to R&B to dancehall. The album starts off with a bang with the opening track 'Cats and Dogs', which is an example of Rae's ability to go off on a fast-paced beat. However, the standout track on the album is 'Kiss Me Back', which is a moody and smooth R&B track that is sure to appeal to fans of the genre. The lyrics on the album are playful and fun, which is in contrast to the more serious sound of some of the other albums on this list. After that, the track list goes through several ups and downs so doesn't always have the same quality throughout.

D **'Buncha Fives' by Buncha:** UK rapper Buncha has made a name for himself with his unique style and hard-hitting beats and albums. His latest album 'Buncha Fives' continues as he has done before and is evidence of his continued ability to create music that is catchy and makes you think. It starts off with the track 'Fast Cars', which immediately sets the tone for the rest of the album with its heavy beats and powerful lyrics (Buncha's lyrics are a mix of social commentary and challenging personal experiences from his youth, making for an interesting listen). Another standout track is 'Old Town', which features interesting lyrics about the struggles of everyday life, much like those he experienced in his childhood. Buncha's vocal delivery on the track is particularly impressive, showing his ability to weave together storytelling and his thoughts on the world around him. He is a rare talent, and a skilled composer and rapper.

Which reviewer:

says that the album is hard to define because the artist covers several different types of music? | 43 |

mentions the differences between this album and previous releases? | 44 |

says that this artist's fans are mainly young people? | 45 |

explains that this album is similar to other albums by this artist? | 46 |

thinks that the album does a good job of balancing quite strong topics with memorable music? | 47 |

suggests that listeners will appreciate the risks this album takes? | 48 |

describes the first release of a rising star? | 49 |

thinks that the artist's difficult time growing up has had a significant impact on their music? | 50 |

suggests that the album has some songs that are better than others? | 51 |

thinks that the music on this album is becoming more grown up and personal? | 52 |

Answer sheet   Test No. ☐

                                                         Mark out of 22 ☐

Name _____   Date _____

Part 5   *6 marks*

Mark the appropriate answer (A, B, C or D).

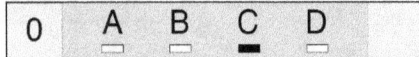

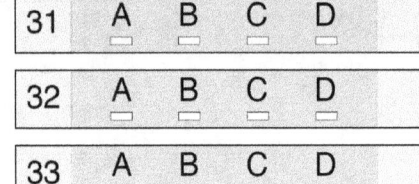   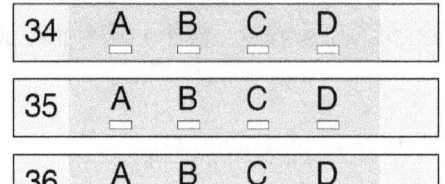

Part 6   *6 marks*

Add the appropriate answer (A–G).

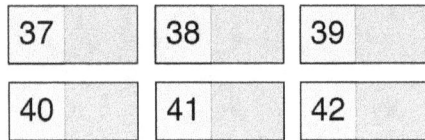

Part 7   *10 marks*

Add the appropriate answer (A, B, C or D).

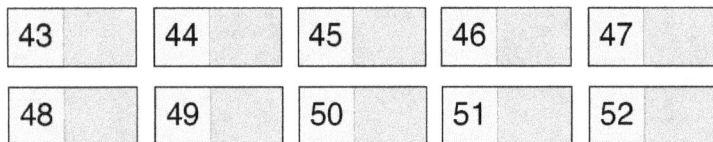

Answers

Cambridge B2 First Reading

Test 1

Part 5		Key words from the questions	Clues from the text
31	D	suggest…meals?	…high in protein-rich foods like lean meat, fish and eggs, carbohydrates and healthy fats…constantly snacking… in between multiple large meals.
32	A	…point about his training does he make…paragraph three?	…take care of your body…take it easy…push yourself to reach your goals.
33	D	his relationships?	but I'm lucky…network of people who understand and support my goals.
34	B	…financial aspects…	…cut down a lot so I wouldn't miss out…I believe it will be worth it.
35	B	feel about his sponsors?	…the partnership benefits us both.
36	C	final paragraph…training and competing…	…not an easy path, but it's incredibly satisfying… sense of achievement…is unmatched…go for it...

Part 6		Key words from the questions	Clues from the text
37	F	That way, they can…keep an open mind…explore a range…	…look into a variety of courses…something that you never thought you'd be interested in...
38	C	…comedy, the science of baking, or oil and gas management…	…look beyond the school curriculum…You can do anything, and not just the typical subjects you learn at school.
39	E	…consider the financial practicalities…	…cost of tuition, accommodation…living expenses…How are you going to get home…How much is rent…how you'll pay for everything...
40	D	…'day in the life' videos by students...	…start doing your research…talk to current students and alumni…the more you know about each course...
41	G	…however…any doubts…listen to those too.	…trust your instincts…it's likely that you've made the right choice…You need to make sure you're making the right decision...
42	A	…look into a range…positives and negatives…consider the practicalities…do your research.	…complex process…careful consideration and research…following these steps…taking the next step

Part 7		Key words from the questions	Clues from the text
43	B	…foreign language…useful skill for travelling?	…incredibly helpful thing for when I go abroad...
44	C	…finds learning…straightforward?	Learning a foreign language has always been a piece of cake for me...
45	D	…learning with others was initially difficult?	…sign up for a course…tricky but also very rewarding…At first, it was challenging…pace of the group...
46	B	…do not have a natural ability for languages?	…some people…pick up languages easily…I'm finding it very challenging. I don't think…comes naturally...
47	C	…errors…part of the learning process?	…tools and techniques…reinforce your learning…don't be afraid to make mistakes!…The more you practise, the better you'll get.
48	C	…essential to develop…routine...	…set aside specific time…the same tools and techniques…reinforce your learning.
49	A	…creates employment opportunities?	…open up new possibilities for work.

Answers

| 50 | A | ...will succeed...self-study? | ...learning one on my own...I'm optimistic that I can do it... |
| 51 | D | ...extra work in addition to lessons...focus? | ...activities outside of class helps me to stay on track. |

Test 2

Part 5		Key words from the questions	Clues from the text
31	A	...become involved in the competition?	...spoke at a school music festival...
32	C	...successful in the competition, the writer needs...	...I have to do everything I can to stand out.
33	D	...made the competition difficult...	...since I've been living out of a suitcase for the past few weeks and travelling here, there and everywhere.
34	B	...make the writer feel...	...incredible achievement and recognition of all the hard work I've put in.
35	C	...'springboard' mean...	...use my win as a springboard to help my career progress.
36	B	...main goal...	...my objective is to make a meaningful impact on the music world...

Part 6		Key words from the questions	Clues from the text
37	D	...fascinating for both dinosaur enthusiasts and sci-fi fans, making it an instant hit.	...the original book, Jurassic Park, written by Michael Crichton in 1990. The novel follows the story of a group of scientists...The book was a success...
38	F	Then there was...made even more money.	...it also made a lot of money.
39	G	After a break, the franchise returned...	...back to the beginning and early ideas...The film features larger and more terrifying...
40	C	However, this time, the risks were higher – audiences were used to the latest technology so the special effects had to better than ever before.	The success of...prompted the filmmakers to make a follow-up...The movie was a hit with fans...
41	E	Therefore, it's no surprise that the franchise is so popular.	...stand out from other monster movies...feel real...
42	A	Its impact on pop culture will undoubtedly continue to entertain readers and movie lovers for generations to come.	In conclusion...set the standard...

Part 7		Key words from the questions	Clues from the text
43	D	...tired of seeing the same thing...	...if you've seen one visitor centre, you've seen them all!...
44	A	...compares...another country?	...Living in a foreign country has definitely been a challenge...
45	A	...wet weather?	...pouring down,...
46	C	...believes...would return to visit...	...I know I would be a regular visitor if I did leave.

Cambridge B2 First Reading

47	B	...earning less money than before?	...be paid little compared to our previous salaries...
48	D	...wants something more exciting...	...saying that I'll miss the close community and how quiet life is (I definitely won't!)...
49	B	...used to be worried and anxious?	...were both feeling stressed...needed a change.
50	A	...don't have much time left...	...I know that I need to leave soon and return to the real world...
51	D	...see the rest of the world?	...looking for jobs where I can be a small fish in a big pond for a change...want to experience new things, meet new people and feel as free as a bird.
52	C	...refreshingly different from most places?	...the sense of 'family' here is incredibly special... there is a strong support system...

Test 3

Part 5		Key words from the questions	Clues from the text
31	A	...afraid of when flying?	...fear of being trapped...out of control...not being able to get out.
32	B	...second paragraph...	...it was initially a good starting point to talk to others who share my same fear, and it helped in many ways...
33	C	...writer's therapist...realise...first sessions?	...Our first session...helped me to understand...my fear was unreasonable...statistically, the chances of something going wrong on a flight were incredibly low.
34	C	...'In following sessions'...line 19?	...we started in small steps...First...then...finally...
35	A	...her flight to Europe?	...techniques I'd been working on for a while... including deep-breathing and positive self-talk...
36	C	How...writer feel...trying to overcome...fear of flying?	...among the most challenging things I've ever done...

Part 6		Key words from the questions	Clues from the text
37	D	They...testing out different strategies...	Governments...thinking up new ways...
38	A	However...avoid using their cars...make a journey on public transport instead.	There are many different ways in which they are doing this...people still settle for using their cars...One example of a government actively promoting public transport...
39	F	At the time, this famous city was one of the most crowded in Europe...long traffic delays...high levels of air pollution.	...London...as a way to reduce traffic congestion...improve air quality...
40	B	...this busy city continued to invest in its subway system...new trains...increasing the frequency of service during peak hours.	...Tokyo...the city also introduced...easier for commuters to plan their journeys...These improvements...even more efficient...
41	C	Other governments...also...new ideas... introducing new technologies and services... more convenient and attractive.	...Tokyo's public transport...For instance, Paris... bike-sharing scheme...model for other cities...
42	G	...this project has been...helped to promote a culture of cycling.	bike-sharing schemes...more than 14,000 bicycles...

Answers

Part 7		Key words from the questions	Clues from the text
43	B	...forms of meditation...exercising your brain?	...practising mindfulness is an excellent way to keep my mind sharp and focused.
44	C	...doesn't mean...stop doing...things that make you happy?	...don't have to give up everything that we enjoy... Although it's true that our bodies and minds may not be as strong as they once were, we can still find joy.
45	D	sociable...lifts your mood...not feeling your best?	...cheer up...a few aches and pains...social club... meeting old friends...
46	A	...activities...physically and mentally healthy...helps you maintain relationships?	Keep active...make the most of the physical activities that you enjoy...stay socially connected...
47	C	...live in the moment...	...slow down and live through each moment...
48	B	...mental and physical health need to be treated equally?	...not just physical health...mental health is just as crucial...
49	D	...play games...connected to friends and family?	...join in with a board game...I started...play puzzles... brought me closer to my daughter.
50	C	...enjoy life...small moments of joy?	...simple pleasures in life...
51	A	...possible and beneficial...new hobbies later in life?	...never too late to start a new activity...active and healthy in your later years.
52	B	...getting rid of pessimistic influences... necessary...	...brings negativity into your life...cut it out...

Test 4

Part 5		Key words from the questions	Clues from the text
31	A	How...live for such a long time?	Despite the advances in modern medicine...are generally unknown.
32	C	First paragraph...writer says that	However, there may be a significantly higher number in reality...
33	B	...fourth paragraph...say about the plane?	...must have been another 40 years...go in one myself...
34	D	Maisie...world wars...	...did what I had to do...made it through.
35	C	...Maisie...modern life?	"...why aren't people remembering that older people deserve respect and aren't all able to access things in the same way as young people are?"
36	A	...Maisie...key to her long life?	"Keep working for as long as you can"...nobody cared...about school or studying...always have a little piece of chocolate every day...something to look forward to!"

Part 6		Key words from the questions	Clues from the text
37	D	Extra dates...added...venues were changed...Frostfire's incredible success...	The gig was the highlight of...recent sell-out, 36-show tour...could never have imagined that she would be stepping out into the spotlight...
38	B	After that initial appearance...social media was in support...soon signed by Aristra Records...a songwriter...ambitious promotional tour.	...auditioning for a well-known TV show...the rest... is history.

Cambridge B2 First Reading

39	F	Nevertheless…world-famous Wembley stadium…final show of the tour.	…original tour…capacity of 12,000…90,000 people attended this arena…
40	A	Fans sang along to every word… amazing atmosphere.	…the crowd was inspired…the energy in the room…incredible…
41	E	…truly standout moments…performed an acoustic version of Wasted Time.	This perfectly created love song…the most played song on every major music platform…
42	G	…gets away with doing other people's songs…	…cover song of Winston Branthorp's 70's classic…

Part 7		Key words from the questions	Clues from the text
43	B	…at risk…dangerous elements and landscapes?	…must pass through rough lands, avoid predators...
44	A	travel from north to south…migration route?	…in the Arctic…move south…coast of Mexico...
45	C	keep future young safe…burying them?	…lay their eggs, which are then covered with small stones to protect…
46	A	help create places to live…other species?	…make new homes for other marine life.
47	C	…use so much energy…cannot live?	…salmon will typically die…physical demands of the journey…too great…to survive...
48	A	make a vital contribution to…survival of other species?	…a crucial part of the global ecosystem.
49	D	…not very active…winter months…time to rest?	…spend the winter months…saving their energy…waiting for the spring...
50	A	…different migration patterns among the species depending on…they live?	…migrations patterns of caribou…depending on the region…where they spend most of their time.
51	D	…a combination of temperature and food options?	…to leave the colder climate, in search of warmer climates and better food sources.
52	B	…move to higher ground during the warmer months?	…summer months…be found at the top of hills…In the winter, they migrate to lower meadows…

Test 5

Part 5		Key words from the questions	Clues from the text
31	B	'these' in line 9…refers to	…consider the cost of living and the quality of education…
32	D	Which is true…decision-making process?	Something deep down just told me I was making the right choice….I decided to trust my initial thoughts and feelings…
33	D	…author say…first few weeks…	…nothing could have prepared me…just how stunning…
34	C	…authors thoughts…lessons?	…teachers…amazing compared to those at home.
35	A	…build her confidence…	…practice my English in real-world situations….actual, everyday situations…helped me to become more confident…
36	B	…decision to study in Ireland?	… The country, people and culture went above and beyond what I'd expected...

Answers

Part 6		Key words from the questions	Clues from the text
37	E	But as the technology improved…pilots became more skilled…dream of transatlantic flight began start becoming a reality.	In the early days…seen as a dangerous task…experts thought was impossible…In fact, history was made in 1919…proving…transatlantic flight was indeed possible.
38	B	This marked a new era in transatlantic travel…more and more people…go up in an aeroplane…travel to distant lands.	…aviation technology continued to change…first transatlantic passenger jet…London to New York…
39	F	…type of aircraft…major breakthrough in aviation technology…high cost…only available to a chosen few.	…the famous Concorde…For most people, faraway travel remained a luxury…only affordable for the wealthy.
40	A	…future of transatlantic flights…many potential developments on the horizon.	One such area of focus and evolution is…
41	C	…promising developments in this regard … use of fuels…natural resources…can reduce carbon emissions…	…environmental impact of air travel….Another option is…
42	D	And yet…a faraway destination such as these…	…it's hard to believe just how far we've come….possible to travel from Bangkok to Barcelona in a matter of hours?

Part 7		Key words from the questions	Clues from the text
43	B	…size…is not…a priority?	I don't need much space – that's not important for me...
44	B	…messy people…less than ideal?	…quite particular about being clean…everyone takes care of their own washing up…important to me.
45	C	…avoid getting on each other's nerves...priority?	…room of their own…avoid any arguments and not annoy each other.
46	A	…might not be able to afford the right property?	…I don't have much of a budget…
47	C	…easy access to the property…key factor?	…good public transport links…transport routes…don't want to end up in a place that's too difficult to get to.
48	D	…change how he originally searched?	…I decided to take a more active approach and asked around…
49	B	…in a hurry to find somewhere?	…don't have much time...
50	A	…change in his relationship?	…recently splitting up with my partner...
51	D	…social connections have been beneficial	…asked a friend who works as an estate agent…we had been approved...
52	B	…car parking…vital element…	…I have a car…important to me that I can park it nearby…

Test 6

Part 5		Key words from the questions	Clues from the text
31	B	…attitude to clearing the attic?	…hugely stressful job...
32	A	…need to do in the near future?	…many trips to charity shops and the recycling centre…next few weeks.
33	D	…find…particularly interesting?	…to my surprise…discovered an antique treasure…jewellery box…complicated details and craftsmanship…no idea who it belonged to…it might be an incredibly valuable treasure.
34	D	…author do with…pictures and letters?	…preserve them…children and my grandchildren.

Cambridge B2 First Reading

		Key words from the questions	Clues from the text
35	D	...author find...carry important memories?	...as well as things that had been passed down to me from my parents and grandparents.
36	A	...final paragraph...author says that	...grateful for the opportunity...

Part 6		Key words from the questions	Clues from the text
37	D	...ancient religious festivals to modern-day parties, light...important role...human cultures throughout history.	...a celebration of human creativity...Today...celebrated worldwide...people from all walks of life...
38	B	...origins of the festival...ancient celebrations...winter solstice...lighting...fires and candles.	These days...Christmas lights...holiday season...
39	F	This festival...celebrated across much of the country...lighting of lamps and candles.	...India...Diwali is also known...welcome success and happiness.
40	A	After they have flown into the air...	...release paper bags lit with candles into the sky...
41	G	While...can be amazing...not to go too far...beauty and entertainment.	...can also come with a significant cost...spend millions of dollars...detailed lighting systems and decorations.
42	C	...high cost...bring together people...all walks of life...beauty of the light displays.	...celebration of human creativity and design...Christmas or Diwali...these festivals...inspire and captivate...worldwide...

Part 7		Key words from the questions	Clues from the text
43	B	...didn't have a lot of technology...early childhood?	...I was a teenager before mobiles and devices took off...
44	A	...human connections benefited...	...my relationships with others improved.
45	D	...hopes they can inspire others...addicted to technology?	...hope...serve as an example to others...similar situation...
46	B	...spend...time...hobby they hadn't done recently?	...played my guitar...first time in months...
47	C	...action...is necessary at times?	...go to extremes sometimes...
48	A	...main digital occupation...playing online games?	As someone who has always been addicted to internet games...
49	C	...technology...responsible for their anxiety?	...keeping me stressed out and anxious...
50	D	...concerned about someone else's use of technology?	...my sister was struggling to put her phone down.
51	C	...their technology...affected...physical health?	...impacting my ability to sleep...couldn't sleep at night...passing out in the middle of the day...
52	A	...try a new activity...	...picked up a new hobby...

Test 7

Part 5		Key words from the questions	Clues from the text
31	A	...her own sleep history...	...a job...I'm passionate about as I know first-hand...impact sleep can have...as a teenager I struggled with insomnia...

Answers

32	D	How…author become a sleep therapist?	…educational background…psychology…went on to study therapy…a one-year course…after completing…formal education, I carried on studying.
33	C	…line 17 'hands-on work' means…	…advising clients with these problems.
34	B	How…therapist help people get better sleep?	…develop plans personal to them…
35	B	What…using…phone before bed?	…can damage sleep in several ways…awaken the brain…harder to get off to sleep.
36	C	What…recommend…good night's sleep?	…engage in stress-free activities…reading a book, taking a warm bath…meditating…

Part 6		Key words from the questions	Clues from the text
37	C	The host country…Japanese skateboarders	…Olympic Games in Tokyo…many locals in the host country.
38	F	In fact,…many of the sport's…	Skateboarding…underground sport with its own subculture…doing what…want…expressing…how they want
39	A	Skaters support each other, even if they are competing against each other…a nice change…other competitive sports.	…skateboarding's informal and relaxed atmosphere…sense of family…This sense of community…skaters often help each other…
40	G	This can include stairs, walls, slides, and other objects and places.	In the street discipline…recreates a real-world street environment…In the park discipline…
41	B	Skateboarders…showed themselves capable of pushing the limits of what is possible…	…remarkable ability…perform at their best…They often came up with new tricks and combinations…both difficult and visually stunning…Watching…a wonderful thing.
42	E	Skaters…express themselves…show their individual personalities…each skateboarder brings something different…	…each skater…own style…each skater's approach to the skate park is unique.

Part 7		Key words from the questions	Clues from the text
43	B	…in the business of buying and selling records?	…owner of a record shop…isn't just a business…stocking the shop…
44	C	…which musicians played on certain albums is interesting…	…real geek about the information provided…spotting who played guitar on the record…that person also played on another favourite album.
45	B	…had to create more space to store their records?	…had to build an extension onto my house…store all my wonderful albums.
46	D	…only recently started collecting vinyl records?	…new to record collecting…vinyl record sleeves covers.
47	A	…looking for new music on vinyl records…play at work?	As a DJ…vinyl record releases…fresh vinyl…ready to play at my next concert.
48	C	…vinyl is much better than…music platforms or services?	…don't get that from a streaming service…always go for a record over a digital download…there's no comparison…
49	B	…into vinyl…both professional and personal…	…isn't just a business—it's a passion…mixing business with pleasure…
50	D	…art and design…is what they're…drawn to	…record covers…most eye-catching designs…as long as the artwork is still in good condition…love for…the artwork…
51	C	…have a good-sized collection after several years?	…collecting…for over a decade now…grown to over 1,000 records.
52	A	…sounds records make, aside from the music…very appealing?	…the warm, vintage sound of a vinyl record. It's not just about the music that comes through!

Cambridge B2 First Reading

Test 8

Part 5		Key words from the questions	Clues from the text
31	C	…area where he works?	…handful of islands around Scotland…
32	D	Why…work as a postman?	…runs in the family…surrounded by the hustle and bustle of my grandparents' village post office…mother and her brothers and sisters…sorting the mail…handling customers…father…
33	A	…how the postal service in Scotland has changed…	…the job requires a lot of physical work…lift heavy packages…
34	B	…line 23, 'made light work of it' means…	…despite the challenges…soon began to…take on more responsibilities.
35	C	…impact…technology…his work?	…reduced the challenges we faced…new technologies…
36	A	What…reason…job satisfaction?	…the pleasure I get…gives me a sense of purpose…proud to do it.

Part 6		Key words from the questions	Clues from the text
37	F	…anybody asking to meet the chef was disappointed.	…mysterious owner, Signor Rossie, had always just gone out…never seemed to be around to talk to customers.
38	D	Expectations for the night were high, but…my experience was a huge let down.	…managed to get myself and a friend tickets for the opening evening…despite being excited to try it out…disappointed from the moment I arrived.
39	G	…looked around the restaurant…decoration made me uneasy.	…walls were painted a horrible shade of red…quickly put together…didn't create the cosy, warm atmosphere…
40	A	…pasta was overcooked…the sauce tasted like it had come out of a can.	The food was the biggest let down of all…so disgusting…hand it back to the server…not that
41	C	…server…uninterested in my table…rarely checked on us…	…the service was incredibly poor…tried to get her attention…she looked annoyed…took her time…
42	E	Whatever the cause…look elsewhere for a quality Italian dining experience.	…can't help but wonder where things went wrong…Was it the quality of the ingredients…lack of attention to detail…bad day for the kitchen staff?

Part 7		Key words from the questions	Clues from the text
43	C	…album is hard to define…artist covers several different genres?	…does not sit in one category…many different influences…from pop to R&B to dancehall.
44	B	…differences between this album and previous releases?	…a departure from their previous work…in contrast to…after the…success of their first…
45	A	…this artist's fans are mainly young people?	…gain a massive following among teenagers…
46	D	…this album is consistent with other albums…	…his unique style…continues as he has done before…his continued ability…
47	A	…the album…good job…balancing quite strong topics…memorable music?	…Despite the fact that…deal with break ups and insecurity…overall sound…fun, fast-paced and songs you'll remember
48	B	…listeners will appreciate the risks this album takes?	Fans will respect this new direction.
49	A	…the first release of a rising star?	…first-ever album…top the charts with her first single…

Answers

50	D	...the artist's difficult time growing up ...significant impact on their music?	...mix of social commentary and challenging personal experiences from his youth...those he experienced in his childhood.
51	C	...the album has some songs that are better than others?	...the track list goes through several ups and downs...doesn't always have the same quality throughout.
52	B	...the music on this album is becoming more grown up and personal?	...more mature side...face up to their own feelings...honest, raw and deeply personal.

Bonus material

The following content is taken from:

Cambridge B2 First Use of English

Test 1

Cambridge B2 First Use of English

Part 1

For questions 1–8, read the text below and decide which answer best fits each gap. In the separate answer sheet, mark the appropriate answer (A, B, C or D).

Getting the right amount of sleep

Do you ever wake up feeling tired and unrested, (1)_____, spending hours in bed? Unfortunately, many people struggle with getting the right amount of sleep, which leads to decreased productivity, mood swings and a host of other health problems.

Getting the right amount of sleep goes hand in hand with a happier and healthier life. Therefore, it's crucial to make the (2)_____ of your time in bed. Establish a bedtime (3)_____, such as reading or meditating, and create a comfortable sleep environment, including a good mattress and black-out curtains.

Catching up on (4)_____ sleep on the weekends can also be helpful, but it's best to (5)_____ oversleeping. Getting too much sleep can (6)_____ your sleep patterns, making it harder to fall asleep at night and leaving you feeling groggy during the day.

Is it possible to wake up every morning feeling (7)_____ and ready to take on the day? The answer is yes! A good night's sleep can make you look like a million dollars, improve your mood and energy (8)_____, and better equip you to handle stress.

1	A	despite	B	although	C	for	D	however
2	A	greatest	B	most	C	easiest	D	majority
3	A	procedure	B	schedule	C	hobby	D	routine
4	A	forgotten	B	heavy	C	lost	D	missing
5	A	discontinue	B	escape	C	avoid	D	ignore
6	A	prevent	B	disrupt	C	remove	D	break
7	A	relieved	B	revised	C	reorganised	D	refreshed
8	A	levels	B	feelings	C	zones	D	measures

Part 2

For questions 9–16, read the text below and decide which word best fits each gap. Use only one word for each gap. In the separate answer sheet, write your answers in capital letters, using one box per letter.

Cloning

Cloning is the process **(9)**_____ producing genetically identical copies of an organism, tissue or cell. In short, cloning consists of three main steps: obtaining genetic material, growing it in a lab and finally transferring it into a host organism.

Although cloning may seem like science fiction, its origins date back to the early 1900s **(10)**_____ scientists first started experimenting with plant cells. **(11)**_____ it wasn't until 1996 that the world was introduced to the first mammal clone, Dolly the sheep.

Scientists have already come up **(12)**_____ a way to clone animals, but before we know it cloning could be used to create new organs, tissues and even whole humans.

Think again if you thought cloning was only limited **(13)**_____ animals. Scientists are already counting **(14)**_____ to revolutionise agriculture by producing crops that are resistant to pests, disease and extreme weather conditions.

In conclusion, cloning is a fascinating field **(15)**_____ has only just begun to scratch the surface of its potential. We can only imagine in our wildest dreams what could be just **(16)**_____ the corner.

Part 3

For questions 17–24, use the stem word on the right to form the correct word that fills each gap. In the separate answer sheet, write your answers in capital letters, using one box per letter.

Street lights

Street lights have been a crucial part of our cities for many years. They play a vital role in **(17)**_____ safety and security during the night. However, the rise in the use of street lights has led to the phenomenon of light pollution, which is becoming a growing concern. — **SURE**

(18)_____, street lighting accounts for a significant portion of a city's energy consumption. This is particularly true in developed cities where street lighting is used **(19)**_____. For example, London spends more than £30 million on street lighting in a single year. These costs are **(20)**_____, and cities must find ways to reduce the amount of energy used by street lighting while still maintaining adequate lighting levels. **(21)**_____, there are many ways in which this can be done. For example, replacing old sodium lights with new LEDs that give off a whiter light for improved **(22)**_____ LEDs are longer lasting and less likely to fail than traditional street lights, so **(23)**_____ costs are also expected to be lower.

ADD

EXTEND

SUBSTANCE

FORTUNE

VISIBLE

MAINTAIN

The goal should be to provide safe and secure lighting for our communities while **(24)**_____ its impact on the environment. — **MINIMUM**

Part 4

For questions 25–30, complete the second sentence, using the word given, so that it has a similar meaning to the first sentence. Do not change the word provided and use between two and five words in total. In the separate answer sheet, write your answers in capital letters, using one box per letter.

25 I thought of a cheap solution to our computer problems.

CAME

I _____ an inexpensive way to solve our computer problems.

26 If you promise to be careful I'll lend you my car.

LONG

I'll lend you my car _____ promise to be careful.

27 We haven't arranged a date for the decorators to come.

BEEN

A date _____ for the decorators to come.

28 We are introducing reduced membership fees that should help those on lower incomes.

INTRODUCTION

_____ new membership fees should help those that earn less.

29 I can help you with the presentation if you want.

MIND

I _____ you with the presentation.

30 "James, do you know what time the meeting starts?" asked Shazia.

IF

Shazia asked James _____ what time the meeting would start.

**Answer sheet: Cambridge B2 First
Use of English**

Test No. ☐

Mark out of 36 ☐

Name _____   Date _____

Part 1: Multiple choice   8 marks

Mark the appropriate answer (A, B, C or D).

| 0 | A | **B** | C | D |

1	A	B	C	D		5	A	B	C	D
2	A	B	C	D		6	A	B	C	D
3	A	B	C	D		7	A	B	C	D
4	A	B	C	D		8	A	B	C	D

Part 2: Open cloze   8 marks

Write your answers in capital letters, using one box per letter.

| 0 | B | E | C | A | U | S | E | | | |

9 ☐☐☐☐☐☐☐☐☐☐☐
10 ☐☐☐☐☐☐☐☐☐☐☐
11 ☐☐☐☐☐☐☐☐☐☐☐
12 ☐☐☐☐☐☐☐☐☐☐☐
13 ☐☐☐☐☐☐☐☐☐☐☐
14 ☐☐☐☐☐☐☐☐☐☐☐
15 ☐☐☐☐☐☐☐☐☐☐☐
16 ☐☐☐☐☐☐☐☐☐☐☐

Part 3: Word formation

8 marks

Write your answers in capital letters, using one box per letter.

17.
18.
19.
20.
21.
22.
23.
24.

Part 4: Key word transformation

12 marks

Write your answers in capital letters, using one box per letter.

25.
26.
27.
28.
29.
30.

Cambridge B2 First Use of English

Test 2

Cambridge B2 First Use of English

Part 1

For questions 1–8, read the text below and decide which answer best fits each gap. In the separate answer sheet, mark the appropriate answer (A, B, C or D).

Wednesday Addams:
The Dark and Quirky Queen of Cool

Wednesday Addams is the ultimate cool girl. She's the gothic, macabre and quirky daughter of Gomez and Morticia Addams from the Addams Family cartoon and movies and has recently been played by Jenna Ortega in a Netflix series.

Due to her gothic style and dark **(1)**_____ of humour, Wednesday has been winning over teens and young adults for generations. Wednesday's fearlessness is something that many teens today can admire. Her independence and willingness to **(2)**_____ authority make her a relatable and inspiring figure.

Even though Wednesday may come **(3)**_____ as a mischievous troublemaker, she has a strong moral compass and always stands up for what she believes in. This is a quality that is all too **(4)**_____ in today's world, and it's what makes Wednesday such a unique and beloved character.

Wednesday Addams is the epitome of cool. She **(5)**_____ independence, non-conformity and the importance of loyalty to your family. Her dark and quirky personality makes her **(6)**_____ out from the rest and has earned her a place in the **(7)**_____ of fans everywhere. So, if you're looking for inspiration and a **(8)**_____ that it's okay to be different, look no further than Wednesday Addams.

1	**A**	type	**B**	quality	**C**	sense	**D**	kind
2	**A**	argue	**B**	support	**C**	challenge	**D**	bother
3	**A**	across	**B**	up	**C**	on	**D**	with
4	**A**	odd	**B**	rare	**C**	few	**D**	ordinary
5	**A**	reflects	**B**	acts	**C**	displays	**D**	represents
6	**A**	look	**B**	sit	**C**	stand	**D**	put
7	**A**	hearts	**B**	eyes	**C**	brains	**D**	stomachs
8	**A**	reminder	**B**	remember	**C**	suggestion	**D**	mention

Part 2

For questions 9–16, read the text below and decide which word best fits each gap. Use only one word for each gap. In the separate answer sheet, write your answers in capital letters, using one box per letter.

The mighty sunflower seed

Sunflower seeds are a great source of healthy fats, protein and vitamins, and they make a delicious snack **(9)**_____ roasted. Here you will find out how to roast sunflower seeds and how to incorporate them **(10)**_____ your cooking.

Many store-bought roasted sunflower seeds can be a rip-off, both in terms **(11)**_____ price and quality. Therefore, roasting your own seeds at home is a great **(12)**_____ to cut out the middleman and enjoy delicious, healthy snacks that **(13)**_____ easy on the wallet.

(14)_____ things first, you'll want to dry out your sunflower seeds. Simply spread **(15)**_____ out on a baking sheet and wait for a day or two.

Once your seeds are dry, it's time to start roasting. Place the seeds in a single layer on a baking sheet. Roast for 10-to-12 minutes or **(16)**_____ the seeds are golden brown.

And there you have it! Roasting sunflower seeds is easy, delicious and healthy. Give it a try, and happy roasting!

Part 3

For questions 17–24, use the stem word on the right to form the correct word that fills each gap. In the separate answer sheet, write your answers in capital letters, using one box per letter.

Greener alternatives to hand wipes

Hand wipes are a ubiquitous item that have a thousand uses, including cleaning and disinfecting hands on the go. Historically, hand wipes have been around for many years, but they have become **(17)**_____ popular in recent years due to several factors. Firstly, the growing **(18)**_____ of the importance of hand hygiene and secondly, for how **(19)**_____ they are when you're unable to access water.

INCREASE
AWARE
CONVENE

Since the outbreak of the Covid-19 pandemic, the demand for hand wipes has **(20)**_____ and they have become a staple in households and public spaces around the world.

RISE

It's important to note that hand wipes are not as **(21)**_____ as hand washing with soap and water, but they can be useful in a pinch when soap and water are not available.

EFFECT

(22)_____, it is important to use environmentally friendly wipes that are biodegradable and free of harsh chemicals. Make sure that you dispose of them in the rubbish bin rather than in your toilet. Aside from the risk to our oceans, waterways and wildlife, water companies spend millions each year **(23)**_____ wet wipes from sewage treatment plants and pumping stations.

ADD

MOVE

Alternatively, washable cloth baby-wipes are now **(24)**_____ available and offer a chemical-free alternative to hand wipes.

READY

Part 4

For questions 25–30, complete the second sentence, using the word given, so that it has a similar meaning to the first sentence. Do not change the word provided and use between two and five words in total. In the separate answer sheet, write your answers in capital letters, using one box per letter.

25 Jamie grew up in England with his grandparents.

RAISED

Jamie _____ his grandparents in England.

26 "Would it be possible to borrow your car?" asked Ade.

LEND

Ade asked _____ her my car.

27 I was told by the doctor that I have to reduce my sugar intake.

DOWN

The doctor told me that I need to _____ the amount of sugar I eat.

28 I wish that I hadn't gone out last night.

REGRET

I _____ last night.

29 You must wear a safety helmet at all times.

WORN

A safety helmet _____ at all times.

30 Otis broke the computer by accident.

MEAN

Otis _____ the computer.

Cambridge B2 First Reading

Notes

Cambridge B2 First Reading

www.ingramcontent.com/pod-product-compliance
Lightning Source LLC
Chambersburg PA
CBHW081918090526
44590CB00019B/3403